AF541248

MANAGEMENT OF ORGANISATIONAL BEHAVIOUR

By

Rajib Lochan Panigrahy

Faculty (MBA), Ambedkar College of Management & Technology, Berhampur, Orissa

&

Anil Kumar Sahu

Reader (MBA), Department of Business Administration, Berhampur University, Berhampur University, Orissa

DISCOVERY PUBLISHING HOUSE PVT. LTD.

NEW DELHI-110 002

Published by:
Tilak Wasan
DISCOVERY PUBLISHING HOUSE PVT. LTD.
4383/4A, Ansari Road, Darya Ganj
New Delhi-110 002 (India)
Phone : +91-11-23279245, 43596064-65
Fax : +91-11-23253475
E-mail : parul.wasan@gmail.com
discoverypublishinghouse@gmail.com
web : www.discoverypublishinggroup.com

***First Edition:* 2012**

ISBN: 978-93-5056-014-3

Management of Organisational Behaviour

Printed at:
Shree Balaji Art Press
Delhi

Preface

The book contains empirical studies of different topics of organizational behaviour. The academicians and researchers who have contributed their articles are well versed with the subject. The articles covered the aspects of behaviour in an organization which are influenced by leadership and motivation that creates, accelerates good morale by developing organizational or industrial culture. A good organizational culture can create good social environment in the organization which strengthen the group towards personal and organizational prosperity.

An organization can develop more commitment, control and acceptance of life's challenges by making a definite decision to be more committed to take control, responsibilities for their own lives and the organization. The hardiness of personality embraces the personality dimension of commitment, locus of control and challenges which neutralizes occupational stress. A hardy personality believes that he has the power to influence, motivate, control to others. It also influences organizational behaviour positively. The hardy personality became exemplary to others for his interest, innovation, interest, importance, truth effort towards his fulfillment to target/commitment in the organization in his relatives and family. In this concern there is a requirement of application of knowledge, inter-personal relationship among personnel and group, employee-employer. The organizational development depends on the application of knowledge, organizational relationship and personal development of workers in the organization. So, it is a pre-requisite in the organization creates personal development, increasing of knowledge and application towards organizational development.

The recognition to employee in his position in several spheres as on the organizational system make them happy and productive which will maintain the organizational commitment and reduce the disturbing elements/aspects of individual, group. Recreation, refreshment, education-training, promotions, deputations, visits and travel, compensations, bonus and incentives, etc. will care of organizational culture, employer-employee relationship, conflict management.

Communication is a tool of Organisational Behaviour which helps for sustainable development of an organization. Hence, participatory communication has prime importance in an organization among individuals, groups, stakeholders, organizations, government, etc. Stress becomes common factor in many organizations especially in corporate sectors. Stress may be in two ways but in the common parlance, stress has been understood in management thought in negative sense. The difficulties, problems at work, gap in communication, drastic behaviour in organization, devastated organizational culture, defective rules in controlling, erratic behaviour of superiors, conflict in organization, defective machinery and other equipments, inefficient or abnormality of co-workers, affects of power and politics, inequalities in HR tools, partialities showing behaviour by managers, etc. made stress on employees which deteriorates employee morale, efficiency, learning attitude, aggressiveness towards organizational development, affects on productivity, increases absenteeism, turnover, negligence to work, etc. that will be a question mark to sustainability of organization instead of prosperity.

Hence, organizational behaviour is an essential tool for management of an organization. The papers contributed by researchers, academicians from the institutions of national repute with elaborations related to organizational behaviour. Hope the piece of work will help the readers, students, researchers and academicians.

Editors

Contents

CHAPTER

A Cultural Construction of an Indian Management Model

*Surya Prakash Pati
**Prof. Pankaj Kumar

ABSTRACT

A nation moving rapidly towards development post liberalization, business organizations are finding it increasingly difficult to ignore the glitter of India resulting in increasing incoming rate of FDIs and outsourcings over the past few years. Added to a relaxed legal framework, the lure of cheap labour is influencing companies to view India as a very favourable business opportunity. However amongst all this euphoria, a question regarding sustainability of such an association cannot be ignored. Hence this chapter tries to construct a management model from a cultural perspective that can be initiated and practiced in the Indian context by the organizations in order to get the optimum out of their employees as well as to tide over the ever increasing competition level. The chapter through theoretical arguments, proposes that a clan culture establishes

* At FPM 09, Indian Institute of Management, Lucknow, Prabandh Nagar, Off Sitapur Road, Lucknow-226013 Uttar Pradesh (India)
** Indian Institute of Management, Lucknow, Prabandh Nagar, Off Sitapur Road, Lucknow-226013 Uttar Pradesh (India)

naturally in the Indian scenario which also encapsulates a weak bureaucracy where the group members' roles, responsibilities and goals are dependent completely on the leader based on the degree of proximity between the two. The chapter also proposes that the leader has to employ a directive style of leadership to get the best out of his/her subordinates since the clan culture is inappropriate to meet the demands of the liberalized economic environment.

Keywords: Indian, clan, directive, management

Introduction

The magnetism of post liberalized India in the world market for labour and investment is unparalleled among the developing nations. Liberalization brought about an improvement in communication as well as information dissemination thus promoting an escalation in the rate of competition. However India still remains influenced by its ancient culture whose origin can be traced to as early as the Indus Valley Civilization (3300 BC). It finds its manifestation in both the personal and professional life of the Indians. Thus it is imperative that industries/organizations take into account this cultural aspect while designing policies in order to gain the optimum from their employees.

Although corporate culture is increasingly being acknowledged by organizational researchers as a source of competitive advantage (Barney 1986, Ott 1989, Pfeffer 1994, Wilkins and Ouchi 1983), yet *building* a corporate culture in isolation from the prevalent national culture is non-viable. This has been supported by findings of Fey and Denison (2003), in which the variability of corporate culture variables in different national cultures has been noticeably established. Then it becomes essential for us to question the validity and applicability of organizational cultural theories in the Indian scenario since most of these theories were conceptualized external to the Indian context. This is in accordance with the thinking of many authors (Adler 1991, Boyacigiller and Adler,

1991) who have extended the above question to many of the organizational theories since a large number of them have witnessed their origin in the US context. Accordingly, taking a cue from the above listed views, we state that the Indian culture is the most important variable that influences management policies and practices in this country. Hence the sustainability, receptivity and effectiveness of every policy or practice are highly dependent on the cultural gelling of the same. Taking cue from our past work and understanding on Indian culture and its effect on management practices (Pati and Kumar, 2009; Pati, *et al.* 2008, Pati and Kumar, 2008) we make an attempt to understand and define a sustainable Indian management model from a cultural standpoint that can effectively steer the economy in the post liberalization scenario.

The architecture of the chapter is as follows. Since we have argued on the supremacy of Indian culture in determining the sustainability of organizational practices and policies in India, initially we try to gather some insights on various aspects of Indian culture. Next we take a quick look at the different types of organizational cultures from a study by Cameron and Quinn (2006) which is followed by theoretical arguments to discover the dominant organizational culture that naturally gets established in the Indian context. An analysis of the current environmental scenario and the effectiveness of the dominant organizational culture in keeping the organization competitively afloat follow next. Finally we present recommendations on the suitability of a leadership style that can bridge the dominant organizational culture with the post liberalized environment of India.

Scope and Guidelines for Investigation

Before we begin exploring into the nature of the interacting variables, it is crucial that we understand and define the expression *management model*. Not only shall it guide us in our search for the precise variables to be employed in the chapter, but also it shall prove beneficial to us in establishing the scope of this undertaking.

The definition of management is closely entwined with its operational aspects namely plan, organize, command, coordinate and control (Fayol, 1916). The above mentioned functions of management form the basis of three distinct yet highly interrelated roles that it has to engage itself in an organization i.e. interpersonal role, informational role and decisional role (Mintzberg, 1973). According to Mintzberg (1973), the interpersonal role of management comprises of figurehead role (ceremonial and symbolic roles), leadership role (hiring, training, motivating and disciplining employees), and liasoning role (contacting external elements to the organization who provide the management with information). Similarly, Mintzberg (1973) asserts that the informational role of the management embraces the roles of monitoring (collection and differentiation of information to external and internal to organization), disseminating (transmission of relevant external information to organizational members), and that of a spokesperson (representation of the organization to external entities). Lastly as propagated by Mintzberg (1973), the decisional role of the management includes the tasks of being an entrepreneur (searching of organization and its environment for opportunities and initiates projects to bring about change), disturbance handler (responsible for corrective action when organization faces important unexpected disturbance), resource allocator (makes or approves significant organizational decisions), and negotiator (responsible for representing the organization at major negotiations).

A decisive look at all the above functions/roles of the management put forth by Mintzberg (1973) prompted us to regroup the above to two distinct clusters, the basis of the above being *exchange and usage of collected information*, that shall present a clearer definition of the management thus serving the purpose of this chapter. We argue that the assemblage of the roles of *monitor, disseminator, disturbance handler, and resource allocator* provide the management a system to integrate all their employees and create an *organizational culture* which in turn outlines the personality of the organization and dictates the reaction of the said organization to various exigencies. The management controls, rather designs, the typology of such a culture by directing the level of and type of information that becomes available to the employees and by channelizing its flow in a specified orientation thus doctoring their responses. Moving in the same direction, we argue that the roles of *figurehead, leader, liaison, spokesperson* and *entrepreneur* agglomerate to form an interface through which the 'shaped' organizational culture interacts with the external environment keeping its competitive advantage intact. This 'interfacial' role of the management can be stated as *leadership style* which is dependent on the amount of external information received and the nature of responses expected from the led culture. To sum up the management may either gather external information and then catalyze the formation of the organizational culture based on the controlled information transmission, or 'create' an organizational culture with well specified response techniques and then modify itself by steering the organization to those environments where the taught response shall prove competitively advantageous. The perspective listed above is in accordance with internal integration and external adaptation theory put forth by Schein (1992).

Therefore a management model in our view consists of two discernible aspects—a *sustainable organizational culture* which shall interact with the external environment on the plank of an *effective leadership style*. Having said this, it becomes evident that our focus must be centred on to decipher the various types of organizational cultures and leadership styles evident in the literature and theoretically establish two different fits in order to decode the Indian management model. The two fits/guiding principles are :

1. Fit between a type of organizational culture and Indian national culture since national culture influences the establishment of the organizational culture (Fey and Denison, 2003).
2. Analytical establishment of an effective leadership style that shall act as an interface between the post-liberalized external environment and the naturally existing organizational culture.

A Look at the Interplaying Variables

Following up from the above discussion, we identify, introduce and define the variables, namely — Indian work culture, organizational culture, and leadership behaviours — whose interaction shall in turn shall help us to characterize the Indian management model.

Aspects of Indian Culture

Sinha and Sinha (1990) and Sinha (1997) have documented five social values that they argue from the basis of Indian culture and affect organizational effectiveness. The five dimensions are listed below :

1. *Affective reciprocity*: This represents the power game in terms of affection (*sneh*) and deference (*shradha*). Those who recognize and submit to power are favoured and those who do not yield to power are discriminated.
2. *Preference for personalized relationship*: This is similar to low masculinity of Kanungo and Mendonca (1996).
3. *Group imbeddedness*: Personalised relationship marks the members of the group and there is a strong 'in-group' and 'out-group' demarcation. Social networking is through own (*apne*)-other (*paraye*) dichotomy.
4. *Duty and obligation over hedonism*: The Hindu religion advocates self-control and containing of impulses.

Moreover *duty* is defined as appropriate role behaviour which again is understood as acknowledgment, promotion and practice of the protection of in-group members and favouring them over others as the principal objective.

5. *Hierarchical perspective*: Indians tend to arrange things, persons, relationships, ideas and almost everything hierarchically. This arrangement is also extended to Indian Gods and reflects in their caste system too. The British too played their part by reinforcing the traditional caste based hierarchical structure (Gopalan and Rivera, 1997). Sinha (1995) has decoded the predisposition of an Indian towards hierarchy in three different dimensions. The first dimension is *status consciousness towards seniors* which advocates obeying, respecting and appeasing the seniors in all possible ways. Anger and hostility towards them is considered disrespectful. The second dimension is *dependence proneness on superior*. This echoes the Indian tendency to seek support, guidance and encouragement from seniors despite being perfectly competent in making decisions. The third and last dimension is the Indians' *preference for personalized relationship* which makes a subordinate expect personal involvement and guidance from his/her superior. The high power distance, status consciousness, centralization of decision making, need to depend upon a patron which in turn results in manifestation of this preference for hierarchy (Sinha, 1997).

These social values have a strong influence on the work culture of Indian managers. While Chhokar (2000) and Sinha (1997) found a high power distance, collectivism and affective reciprocity as the major traits in Indian managers, Hofstede (1980) rates Indian managers high on uncertainty avoidance.

Organizational Culture

As mentioned previously, the second important player in this analysis is the variable of organizational culture. Schein (1992) defines corporate culture as 'a pattern of shared basic beliefs that the group learned as it solves its problems of external adaptation and internal integration that has worked well enough to be considered valid, and therefore to be taught to new members as the correct way to perceive, think, and feel in relation to those problems'. He views culture in three tiers. The first tier that is most markedly palpable to outsiders is the *visible artifacts* which are associated with physical features of work environment. The second tier is the *espoused values* and is explicitly articulated and often expressed by the organization's mission statement. And finally, the third tier that constitutes the underlying beliefs comprising of unexpressed and unconscious *assumptions* shared by the organization's members which guide thinking, and suggest ways in which problems are addressed.

Despite the complexity and bewilderment that shadows the concept of organizational culture, American researchers Kim S. Cameron and Robert E. Quinn developed a theoretical model, referred to as the Competing Values Framework (Cameron and Quinn, 2006) that helps in improved comprehension of the organizational culture construct. The model is based on several indicators of organizational effectiveness, which can be differentiated from each other by two dimensions. The interaction of these dimensions result in four distinct cultures to which organizations can be grouped to (Fig. 1.1). These two dimensions are listed below :

- *Internal* vs. *External Orientation:* While the former indicates a focus on the internal affairs of the organization bringing about unity and integration, the later refers to attending on the external affairs of the organization i.e. competition and differentiation.
- *Stability and Control* vs. *Flexibility and Discretion:* While the former indicates an interest in keeping things

unchanged, the later refers to an interest in designing changes.

Fig. 1.1 gives the four types of cultures that originate from the interaction of the effectiveness parameters — *clan, adhocracy, market and hierarchy*. A brief description of each of these organizational culture types is given below :

	Flexibility and Discretion	
	Clan	Adhocracy
Internal Orientation		External Orientation
	Hierarchy	Market
	Stability and Control	

Fig. 1.1 : The Competing Values Framework (Cameron and Quinn, 2006)

Clan culture: These types of organizations resemble with extended families that have shared values and goals. Stability and long term commitment constitute the fundamental principles behind their existence. The employees are committed to the company (loyalty) as well as the company to its employees (security). The work is done by teams who may have quite autonomous roles and the customers are seen as partners. *Involvement* of all employees is the characteristic of these organizations (Denison, 1990).

Adhocracy culture: In adhocracy culture, the organizations are predisposed to flexibility in their functionalities in accordance with the alteration in the environment. Employees are motivated and expected to be innovative, creative, and entrepreneurial. No centralised authority or actor exercises power and every individual is free to act depending on the external environmental contingencies. Denison (1990) characterises them as high *adaptable* cultures.

Market culture: The activities of a market culture has an external orientation, however unlike the culture of adhocracy, it also comprises the characteristic of centralization of power. This is because these organizations, being very clear about their customer base, are committed to meet their demands thus acquiring them permanently. Profitability and market shares, for example, are the lens through which the effectiveness of this type of company is viewed. Therefore the main values are competitiveness and productivity, which are measured both between the organizational units as well as between individuals. A sense of *mission* with control permeates these organizations (Denison, 1990).

Hierarchy culture: These types of organization often rely on formal structures, policies and procedures to keep things on the trot. Their internal focus, according to Denison (1990), is on *consistency*.

Leadership Behaviours

Finally we arrive at the interfacial part of the management model construct that we had conceptualized previously i.e. the *leadership style*. Two types of leadership behaviours are primarily differentiated by numerous leadership models — the 'task-oriented' and 'relationship oriented' behaviour. Various authors have also phrased them as 'initiating-structure' and 'consideration' respectively (Judge, Piccolo & Ilies 2004). Some others, on the other hand, have coined them as 'directive' and 'supportive' leadership respectively (Northouse 2004). These two leadership dimensions have received substantial attention in cross-cultural studies (Peterson & Hunt 1997; Dorfman 2004). Although research on leadership has progressed beyond the dual dimensions of 'task' and 'relationship oriented' behaviours, yet many authors still trust the robustness of the model to be of use in contemporary times (Yukl, 2002; Northhouse 2004; Judge et. al. 2004).

A strong tendency to control discussions, dominate interactions, and an exhibition of personal direction towards task completion marks 'directive leadership' behaviour (Cruz, Henningson, & Smith, 1999). In addition to above, time management, pressure to realize targets, and a close supervision of details are viewed as characteristics of this style (Schmidt & Yeh, 1992). Directive leader behaviour puts the team members on a dependent role forcing them to wait for the manager's approval before applying themselves, which in turn pushes them to lessen their initiatives and dampens their motivation for extra activities.

On the contrary, the 'supportive leadership' style has been defined and used since the 50s of the 20th century. Definitions usually emphasize on sensitivity to team members' needs (House, 1971). A team climate is noticeable in which members feel empowered to act and collaborate with each other. The manager facilitates the empowered team members with trust and support which in turn helps the team members to take initiative, reciprocate the behaviour by supporting team members, and overcome fears of criticism (Euwema, Wndt & Van Emmerik 2007).

The Theory of Indian Management Model

Having stated and discussed above the chief variables that shall help us in formulating the theory, we revisit the guidelines established earlier to help us proceed plausibly in constructing the Indian Management Model.

The Clan Culture as the Natural Corporate Culture in Indian Context

Moving along the first guideline that vouches for a fit between a typology of an organizational culture and the Indian national culture we make an attempt in this section to theoretically correlate the various aspects of Indian national culture as put forth by Sinha and Sinha (1990) and Sinha (1997) to various organizational cultures proposed by Cameron and Quinn (2006). The objective of the entire endeavour is to ascertain the organizational culture that shall flourish naturally in the Indian context.

A strong in-group/out-group orientation in the Indian cultural context symbolizes that relations will always be preferred over strangers and shall be showered with favours due or undue, which in turn shall endorse barriers to entry of external entities thus minimizing dilution of the in-group culture. This choice of relations over strangers also reinforces the strengthening of the parameters of bonding, for e.g. a common set of socio-cultural beliefs and behaviours used in self-identification and as a cognitive leash, which in fact is a very significant requisite for the establishment of a clan culture (Chan, 1997) which in turn further ensures the establishment of a strong differentiation of the clan from its external environment thus promoting the building of a defensive wall against external instability in order to attain the level of self sufficiency (isolationaism) (Chan, 1997). Affective reciprocity goes forward to facilitate the established cohesiveness and the internalization of we/they mentality that originated on account of the in-group/out-group differentiation. Additionally, we argue, it also reinforces the belief in the importance of individual clan member, which in turn reinforces internal stability, the fundamental facet of a clan culture and hence contributes towards strengthening the clan identity which is further fortified by group imbeddedness since it enforces the belief, acceptance and strict distinction of traditions, rituals, rites and heroes/heroines of the clan which are to be protected at all costs. Finally the aspect of status consciousness towards seniors ensures 'loyalty' of group members towards their leader which is exchanged with 'security' provided by the leader to them in the garb of personalized relationship and guidance that defines and secures a mutual long term commitment between them thus promoting and strengthening the establishment of a clan culture. To sum up, the Indian social values of affective reciprocity, personalized relationship and group imbeddedness will promote, create and support a clan culture to thrive naturally in the organization having Indian employees.

Moving further, we also argue that the preference of the Indians for self-control over hedonism is primarily responsible in promotion of hierarchy since it limits them from independent thinking and instigates them to seek the advice of superiors. Self-control demarcates a span of action and control thus forcing the Indians to religiously limit themselves within the created boundary which in turn endorses the creation of a hierarchy, where each hierarchical level operates within its self-created boundary. We extend the argument in stating that this also decreases their risk taking ability since it shall be viewed as encroachment to another's hierarchically created territory which may not be viewed encouragingly. This is supported by Hofstede's (1980) study where he rates India high in uncertainty avoidance. This hierarchical orientation or 'looking up' at the superior, contributes a formal hierarchical culture to the Indian organization where processes are dictated by the superior or source of power. This argument is reinforced when one considers that high power distance is a prominent feature of Indian culture (Chhokar, 2000; Sinha, 1997). However we hold the view that this hierarchical culture is at the mercy of the clan culture and the processes, rules and the actors at various hierarchies can be altered depending on the motive of the source of power and the degree of personalized relationship one has with him/her. The above statement can be understood in better light when one considers the Indian definition of 'duty', i.e. favouring the in-group members over others. Thus collectivism is high but that need not result in performance. The argument above has empirical support from the studies of Pati, *et al* (2008) and Pati and Kumar (2009). Hence rules and procedures are overlooked when it threatens group imbeddedness and loyalty to superiors thus contributing to an inconsistent hierarchical culture.

Need of the Hour—Conversion of Clan Culture to Market Culture

The year 1991 brought to a close a long era of socialist policies in India. Political analysis suggests that the size and scope of the liberalisation reforms which ensued were largely unexpected. Up to this point the Central Government control over industrial development was maintained through public ownership, licensing and other controls. Moreover, industrialisation was planned and took place in highly protected environment which was maintained by high tariff, non-tariff barriers and controls on foreign investment. The New Industrial Policy introduced in 1991 shattered this old order with a distinct focus on trade, liberalisation and deregulation. It opened a large number of industries for automatic approval of foreign technology agreements and to foreign investment of up to 51 per cent of equity. A Foreign Investment Promotion Board was also established to consider proposals of up to 100 per cent equity. These policy reforms were followed by a dramatic rise in the number of approvals of foreign collaboration and actual foreign direct investment flows showed a similar marked increase.

The large scale deregulation drive also ensured the large-scale removal of industrial licensing. Under the Industries (Development and Regulation) Act of 1952, firms were required to apply for an industrial licence from a Licensing Committee in order to set up a new production unit, expand capacity by more than 25 per cent of existing levels or manufacture a new product. These requirements were removed for the majority of industrial sectors in 1991. Similarly, the New Industrial Policy saw a substantial reduction in the number of industrial categories reserved for the public sector from 17 to 8 in 1991 and to 6 in 1993.

Bolwjin and Kumpe (1992) evaluated the market demands which most post industrial organizations are confronted with. We argue that their study can be applied to understand the Indian scenario post liberalization. According to their findings, modern organizations are confronted with four important performance standards — innovation, flexibility, quality, and efficiency. van Muijen and Koopman, (1994) added a few more standards like 'kaizen', less absenteeism, less obsolescence of knowledge and fewer turnovers. Thus the above standards call for a larger span of commitment of organization members which is not limited to their task alone. This advocates a redesign of tasks (more autonomous, more competitive), reframing of organization structure (flat, delegation, business units) and a rethink on applied leadership styles.

So is a clan cultured Indian organization suitable enough to meet the required performance standards listed above to compete in the post-liberalized and globalized scenario? The current discussion is focussed to answer the above stated question. Although involvement of all employees (Denison, 1990) is the trademark of a clan culture with independent and autonomous teams committed to the organization, yet the Indian definition of 'appropriate role behaviour' shall seriously hamper the organizational performance. As argued previously, collectivism is paramount yet need not convert in performance since internal stability is the fundamental basis of this culture. So all out effort is directed to keep the group intact than usage of the same in achievement of significant results. Defence of the honour and existence of the clan is more crucial. Besides, hierarchy and degree of personalized relationship trigger a tendency to form multiple clans at every hierarchical level proportionately with the expansion of the organization. So loyalty of a clan member is directed predominantly towards the leader of the hierarchical circle he/she belongs to. The above thought is in accordance with the findings of Pati and Kumar (2009) who assert that Indian workers exhibit person-centric commitment predominantly;

their organizational commitment is largely a function of the 'emotional distance' they are from their leader. Thus values may be shared within a clan but not across clans which will result in less cooperation within clans/departments thus hampering innovation. Further the non-independent nature of an individual in a clan owing to compulsory adherence to a set of rules framed by the leaders of the clan leaves little scope for flexibility and independent opinion. Hence the definitions of quality and efficiency are preset and doctored which may be completely orthogonal with respect to super ordinate goal of the organization. Either there shall be underperformance with non-optimal usage of resources or over-performance with rapid depletion of resources. A lack of unifying system shall thus reduce the organization to an aggregation of uncooperative clans. Hence the clan culture is ruled to be inappropriate in competitive positioning of the organization.

A revisit to Cameron and Quinn (2006) shall reveal that an organization requires either adhocracy or market culture to innovate with speed without strict quality control in place to effectively compete in the current environmental conditions prevailing in India. Developing a culture of adhocracy is difficult in Indian context, given the employees' high degree of uncertainty avoidance and dependence proneness on superiors. Moreover there is a sense of self-control which may stop them from being freely and responsibly innovative. The intrinsic urge to belong to a group may also act as a controlling factor in letting go of the entrepreneurial spirit.

On the other hand, the market culture can be developed provided an appropriate interface/catalyst is provided. The conversion of the clan culture to a market culture comprises the rest of the discussion.

Directive Leadership Style as the Necessary Interface

We arrive at the final aspect of the management model construct that we had conceptualized in the beginning of this discussion i.e. evaluating and establishing an effective leadership style that shall steer the organization in the current environmental demands. With a strategic emphasis on market superiority initiated by the motive of competitive advantage, the primary goal of a market culture is an efficient production mechanism focussed on quality deliverance in specified time. Thus it requires the orientation of all clans/department to a unified purpose with a central authority overseeing the integration and specifying the parameters of quality that each clan/department has to meet and is measured from the yardstick of the required final product.

Noting the requirements above, and standing on the shoulders of the studies by Pati and Kumar (2009) and Pati and Kumar (2008), we affirm that a clan cultured organization to be effective in the currently prevalent economic environment of India requires its management to assume a directive style of leading. In the Indian context the development of a market culture is arguably easy, for the need to control and dominate over his subordinates, that are the primary facets of directive leadership, can be done away with by the leader for he is already given the due respect and status owing to the dimension of status consciousness towards seniors as mentioned earlier (Sinha, 1995). Moreover the Indians' obsession with self-control and personal guidance will free the leader from excessive controlling. The leader in this context only need fix well defined goals and targets, develop a personal relationship with his subordinate as far as possible and communicate the deliverables unequivocally to them. Pati and Kumar (2008) further emphasize that for maximizing the creative gain from the employees, the leader need focus only on goal setting, leaving the process to be chalked out by the subordinates. However we hold the view that the directive style of leadership should be employed after a personal relationship is established with the subordinates. This is in accordance with Hennessey's (1998) argument that ability to understand and work within a culture is a prerequisite to effective leadership. In absence of personal relationship, the leader may be obeyed owing to his/her hierarchical position, but the values of the organization may not be transferred or appreciated by the subordinate thus leading to disengagement from their assigned role.

A Research Framework and Propositions

Summing up the entire discussion, we provide a framework and two propositions on an effective performance oriented Indian management model in the current economic scenario. The framework, represented in Fig. 1.2, shows the interplay of social values, as argued before to create a spontaneously existing corporate culture and the required leadership style to steer such an organization in a competitive scenario that is prevalent post 1991.

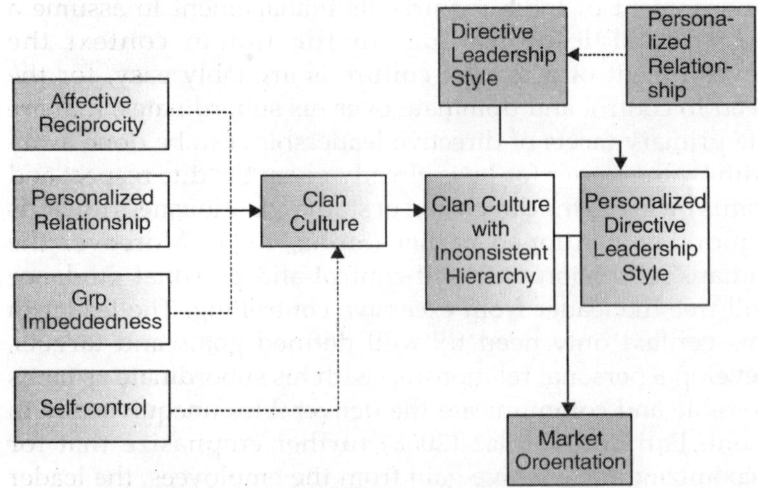

Fig. 1.2 : A Proposed Framework of Indian Management Model

Based on the above framework two propositions can be decoded that explains an effective Indian management model in the current scenario:

Proposition 1 : The Indian social values promote the creation and existence of a clan culture in an organization which may in turn accommodate an inconsistent hierarchical culture.

Proposition 2: In the Indian context, a directive leadership style can effectively steer the organization, however it should be employed after establishing a personalised relationship with the subordinates.

Conclusion

An attempt to construct an Indian management model has been made in this chapter. In short, the effective Indian management model in the post-liberalized economic scenario can be stated as loosely hierarchical clan culture led by a directive leader. With numerous multinationals coming into the nation post liberalization, this model can be of use to them to design their organizational structure and putting the right people in the right position.

References

Adler, N. J., (1991), *International Dimensions of Organizational Behaviour*, 2nd ed, Kent Publishing, Boston, MA

Barney, J. B., (1986), 'Organizational Culture: Can It Be a Source of Sustained Competitive Advantage?', *Academy of Management Review*, Vol.11, pp. 656-665.

Boyacigiller, N. A., and Adler,N.J., (1991), 'The Parochial Dinosaur: Organizational Science in a Global Context', *Academy of Management Review*, Vol. 16, No. 2, pp. 262-290

Bolwjin, P. T., and Kumpe, T. (1992), 'Marktgericht ondernemen: Management van continuiteit en verneiuwing' in van Muijen, J. J., Koopman, P. L., (1994), 'The Influence of National Culture on Organizational Culture: A Comparative Study Between 10 Countries', *European Work and Organizational Psychologist*, Vol. 4, No. 4, pp. 367-380.

Cameron, K. S., and Quinn, R. E., (2006), *Diagnosting and Changing Organizational Culture*, Revised Edition, JosseyBass, US.

Chan, A., (1997), 'Corporate Culture of a Clan Organization', *Management Decision*, Vol. 35, No. 2, pp. 94-99.

Note: The authors wish to acknowledge the help of Ms. Prajna Srutismara in proof reading and formatting the chapter.

Chhokar, J. S., (2000), 'Effective leadership in India: A Multi method Study', in Kumar, M. R., and Sankaran, S., (2007), 'Indian Culture and the Culture of TQM: A Comparison', *The TQM Magazine*, Vol. 19, No. 2, pp. 176-178.

Cruz, M. A., Henningson, D. D., and Smith, B. A. (1999), 'The Impact of Directive Leadership on Group Information Sampling, Decisions, perceptions of the Leader' in Euwema, M. C., Wendt, H. & Van Emmerik, H. (2007), 'Leadership Styles and Group Organizational Citizenship Behaviour Across Cultures', *Journal of Organizational Behaviour*, Vol. 28, pp. 1035-1057.

Denison, D., (1990), *Corporate Culture and Organizational Effectiveness*, New York: John Wiley & Sons.

Dorfman, P. W., (2004), 'International and Cross-cultural Leadership Research' in Euwema, M. C., Wendt, H. & Van Emmerik, H. (2007), 'Leadership Styles and Group Organizational Citizenship Behaviour Across Cultures', *Journal of Organizational Behaviour*, Vol. 28, pp. 1035-1057.

Euwema, M. C., Wendt, H., and Van Emmerik, H. (2007), 'Leadership Styles and Group Organizational Citizenship Behaviour Across Cultures', *Journal of Organizational Behaviour*, Vol. 28, pp. 1035-1057.

Fayol, H. (1949), *General and Industrial Administration*, London, Pitman.

Fey, C. F., and Denison, D. R. (2003), 'Organizational Culture and Effectiveness: Can American Theory Be Applied in Russia?' *Organizational Science*, Vol. 14, No. 6, pp. 686-706.

Gopalan, S., and Rivera, J. B., (1997), 'Gaining a perspective on Indian Value Orientations: Implications for Expatriate Managers', *International Journal of Organizational Analysis*, Vol. 5, No. 2, pp. 156-179.

Hofstede, G., (1980), *Culture's Consequences: International Differences in Work- related Values*, Sage, Thousand Oaks, CA.

House, R. J., (1971), 'A Path-goal Theory of Leader Effectiveness', *Administrative Science Quarterly*, Vol. 16, pp. 321-339.

Judge, T., A., Piccolo, R. F., and Ilies, R., (2004), 'The Validity of Consideration and Initiating Structure in Leadership Research' in Euwema, M. C., Wendt, H., and Van Emmerik, H. (2007), 'Leadership Styles and Group Organizational Citizenship

Behaviour Across Cultures', *Journal of Organizational Behaviour*, Vol. 28, pp. 1035-1057.

Kanungo, R. N., and Mendonca, M., (1996), 'Cultural Contingencies and Leadership in Developing Countries', in Kumar, M R., and Sankaran, S., (2007), 'Indian Culture and the Culture of TQM: A Comparison', *The TQM Magazine*, Vol. 19, No. 2, pp. 176-178.

Mintzberg, H., (1973), *The Nature of Managerial Work*, Prentice Hall, New Jersey.

Northouse, P. G., (2004), 'Leadership Theory and Practice', in Euwema, M. C., Wendt, H., and Van Emmerik, H. (2007), 'Leadership Styles and Group Organizational Citizenship Behaviour Across Cultures', *Journal of Organizational Behaviour*, Vol. 28, pp. 1035-1057.

Ott, J. S., (1989), *The Organizational Culture Perspective*, Dorsey Press, Chicago, IL.

Pati, S. P., and Kumar, P., (2008), 'Barriers to Creativity: An Investigation of Its Dimensions in the Indian Context', Paper Presented at the *3rd Conference on Global Competition and Competitiveness of Indian Corporates,* Indian Institute of Management, Lucknow, India, May 29-31.

Pati, S. P., Padhi, M., and Kumar, P., (2008), 'Psychological Empowerment: Investigation into the Reliability of Its Conceptualization in the Indian Context and an Exploration into the Influence of the Dimensions of Barriers to Creativity on the Same', Paper Presented in *XVIIIth Annual Conference of National Academy of Psychology (NAOP)*, Indian Institute of Technology Guwahati, India, Dec 14-17.

Pati, S. P., and Kumar, P., (2009), 'Organizational Commitment: An Exploration of Its Morphology in the Indian Context' in S. C. Das (Ed.), *Service Centric Strategy and Market Dynamics*, pp. 291-301, Kanishka Publishers, New Delhi.

Peterson, M. F., and Hunt, J. G., (1997), 'International Perspectives on International Leadership', *Leadership Quarterly*, Vol. 8, pp. 203–223.

Pfeffer, J., (1994), *Competitive Advantage Through People: Unleashing the Power of Work Force*, Harvard Business Press, Boston, MA

Schein, E., (1985), *Organizational Culture and Leadership*, Jossey – Bass, San Francisco, CA.

Schmidt, S. M., and Yeh, R. S. (1992), 'The Structure of Leader Influence, A Cross-national Comparison', *Journal of Cross-Cultural Psychology*, Vol. 23, pp. 251-264.

Sinha, J. B. P., and Sinha, D. (1990), 'Role of Social Values in Indian Organizations', *International Journal of Psychology*, Vol. 25, Nos. 5/6, pp. 705-714.

Sinha, J. B. P., (1995), 'The Cultural Context of Leadership and Power', in Kumar, M. R., (2007), 'Assessment of Hierarchical Tendency in an Indian Bureaucracy', *International Journal of Public Sector Management*, Vol. 20, No. 5, pp. 380-391.

Sinha, J. B. P., (1997), 'A Cultural Perspective in Organizational Behaviour in India', in Kumar, M. R., and Sankaran, S. (2007), 'Indian Culture and the Culture of TQM: A Comparison' *The TQM Magazine*, Vol. 19, No. 2, pp. 176-178.

Wilkins A., and Ouchi, W. G. (1983), 'Efficient cultures: Exploring the Relationship Between Culture and Organizational Performance', *Administrative Science Quarterly*, Vol. 28, pp. 468-481.

van Muijen, J. J., Koopman, P. L., (1994), 'The Influence of National Culture on Organizational Culture: A Comparative Study Between 10 Countries', *European Work and Organizational Psychologist*, Vol. 4, No. 4, pp. 367-380.

Yukl, G., (2002), *Leadership in Organizations*, in Euwema, M. C., Wendt, H. and Van Emmerik, H. (2007), 'Leadership Styles and Group Organizational Citizenship Behaviour Across Cultures', *Journal of Organizational Behaviour*, Vol. 28, pp. 1035-1057.

CHAPTER

Hardy Personality

*Dr. Subhashree Panda

ABSTRACT

The good news is that we too can become 'hardy' personalities and that we can teach our children how to develop 'hardy' personalities. All it takes is a paradigm shift in our thinking methods. We must understand that life and the changes and stress associated with it must be managed, not by avoiding it but by bolstering our response to it. We too can develop more commitment, control and acceptance of life's challenges by making a definite decision to be more committed, to take control and responsibility for our own lives and by fairly and squarely facing the changes and challenges life brings.

"You can't always influence what others may say or do to you but you can influence how you react and respond to it."

(Unknown)

Research has shown that some people are more resistant to stress and better able to cope with it than others. This is partly

* Lecturer, Department of Business Administration, North Orissa University, Baripada, Orissa.

due to the fact that some people have a number of personality traits that protect them from the effects of stress; psychologists call this the stress-hardy personality. One researcher in the stress hardiness field is clinical psychologist at the City University, New York, Doctor Suzanne Kobosa. In the late 1970s she carried out a study on a group of executives who were under a lot of stress whilst their company, the Bell Telephone Company in the USA, was undergoing radical restructuring. On completion of the study, when the data was analysed, she found that certain personality traits protected some of the executives and managers from the health ravages of stress.

The construct labelled as *Hardiness* in the 1970s by Suzanne Kobosa (1979), an American behavioural scientist, identified a collection of personality characteristics that neutralize occupational stress. This collection of characteristics, referred to as hardiness, involves the ability to perceptually or behaviourally transform negative stressors into positive challenges. Hardiness embraces the personality dimensions of *commitment, locus of control,* and *challenge.* Kobosa characterized the 'hardy personality' as one that encompasses high levels of commitment or involvement in day to day activities, the perception that one has control over life events, and a tendency to view unexpected change as a challenge rather than a threat to a well-being.

Hardy personalities exhibit the following characteristics:

- **Commitment :** Commitment reflects the extent to which an individual is involved in whatever he or she is doing. Committed people have a sense of purpose and do not give up under pressure. The hardy person believes in the truth, importance and interest of who she is and what she is doing. Hardy people have a strong commitment to self, work, family and other values and are often role models for their children and their community.

- **Control :** A hardy person believes that she has the power to influence the course of events in her life, even unpleasant events, and she accepts personal responsibility for both the failures and successes in her life. Individuals with internal locus of control believe they can influence the events that affect their lives. People possessing this trait are more likely to foresee stressful events, thereby reducing their exposure to anxiety producing situations. Studies have shown that how much control we perceive we have over any stressor will influence how difficult the stressor will be for us to cope with. Researchers have found there are basically two types of control, Internal and External, and these can either exacerbate or reduce a stressful situation.

Internal Locus of Control

With the internal locus of control people are aware that they cannot influence all the external events that go on in their lives, but they do have a deep sense that they have a choice in how they react to that stressor and believe that although they cannot totally influence it, they do have some influence over the event.

External Locus of Control

In the external locus of control people believe that they have little or no control over what happens to them; what happens is due to fate or destiny and that they will not be able to influence it. For example, someone who suffers a chronic back problem may believe it is their destiny and fate in life to suffer the pain. They may believe there is nothing they can do to influence their condition and the subsequent pain, so therefore they do not take any action, nor use any strategies that could enable them to reduce their pain.

In life it is impossible to remove all the pressure and stress that we will encounter, but that doesn't mean we are impotent in the face of it. By learning stress management strategies we can influence how these events affect us, even though we cannot remove them. For example, in one study researchers looked at two groups of people who were under stress. One group practised relaxation regularly and the other group did not. The research data revealed that, although both groups had higher levels of stress hormones, the group that practised relaxation showed less effects of these stress hormones on their organs and systems when compared to the group who did not practice relaxation.

We do have some degree of control over how stressors affect us. The late Dr Viktor Frankyl, a psychiatrist who was a prisoner in the Nazi concentration camp at Auschwitz, said the one thing that you cannot take away from a person is their choice of how they deal with the difficult situations which they find themselves in.

In managing our stress its important to recognise where our locus of control is and with time, stress management training and practice we can move from an external locus of control to a more internal locus of control and in so doing improve our coping abilities.

Challenge : Challenge is represented by the belief that change is a normal part of life. Hardy people see change in their lives as a challenge, not a threat. Change is seen as an incentive for further growth and is responded to by accepting the unexpected, exploring the environment and discovering which resources to approach and use when needed.

Although this construct would appear to be highly salient to strain reactions, there has been relatively little investigations of its role in job stress. Kobosa and her colleagues' research on the impact of hardiness on strain in general found that hardy persons tended to report fewer illnesses and higher levels of general well-being (e.g., Kobosa, 1982), although some other studies have failed to replicate this finding. it has been suggested that the positive link between hardiness and health arises because hardy individuals have more adaptive cognitions concerning stressors than do their less hardy counterparts and that these cognitions are reflected in lower levels of physiological arousal under conditions that might be stressful (Allred & Smith, 1989)

Direct investigations of the relationship between hardiness and indicators of strain, including physiological measures, have not consistently confirmed a stress buffering effect of hardiness (Benishek & Lopez, 1997). For instance, Allred and Smith (1989) assessed both cognitive and physiological responses of high and low hardiness individuals in a challenging situation that presented either high or low threat to their self concept. There was evidence that hardy persons experienced less psychological strain than their non-hardy counterparts, but no moderating effect of hardiness was obtained with respect to physiological outcomes, a finding that calls into question the presumed linkage between hardiness and physical health.

A five year study of 259 managers from a public utility revealed that hardiness—commitment, locus of control, and challenge-reduced the probability of illness following exposure to stress. Hardy individuals interpreted stressors less negatively and were more likely to use control coping strategies than unhardy people. Furthermore additional research demonstrated that hardy individuals displayed lower stress, burnout and psychological distress and higher job satisfaction than their less hardy counterparts. Research findings indicate that person high in hardiness report better health than those low in hardiness, even when they encounter major stressful life changes (Oulette-Kobasa & Puccetti, 1983). Finally, a study of 73 pregnant women revealed that hardy women had fewer problems during labour and more positive perceptions about their infants than unhardy women.

Roth, Wiebe, Fillingham, and Shay (1989) obtained self ratings of health symptoms from their respondents but also failed to demonstrate that hardiness either was directly associated with self reported health or moderated the impact of stressful life experiences on illness ratings. More recently, Benishek and Lopez (1997) examined gender differences in frequency and severity of 'life stress' scores and examined the moderating influence of hardiness on the relationship between life stressors and self reported health in men and women. This study identified a hardiness buffering effect only in male respondents. The researchers suggested that men may be more likely to use hardiness related problem focussed coping strategies that override the deleterious impact of stressors in their lives, whereas women may be more likely to use emotion focussed coping that addresses the consequences rather than the stressors themselves. Further work is needed to confirm this speculation.

One practical offshoot of this research is organizational training and development programmes that strengthen the characteristics of commitment, personal control, and challenge. Because of cost limitations, it is necessary to target key employees or those most susceptible to stress. The hardiness concept also meshes nicely with job design. Enriched jobs are likely to fuel the hardiness components: commitment and challenge. Employees scoring low in hardiness would be good candidates for stress-reduction programmes.

In summary, although the concept of hardiness and its proposed impact on the experience of strain has intuitive appeal, to date evidence to support its effects has been somewhat disappointing. Furthermore there have been suggestions that the hardiness construct is too global and that further research should examine the three specific components more closely (Hull et al., 1987; Roth et al., 1989) especially, the commitment component. At this point, there is a lack of substantive evidence that hardiness demonstrates a consistent moderating effect on ether psychological well-being or physical health. Its influence in fact is due to other mechanisms especially the forms of appraisals undertaken by individuals confronting stressors.

References

Kreitner Robert, Kinicki Angelo & Buelens Marc, *Organisational Behaviour*, Mc Graw Hill Publication Limited, New Delhi, 1999, pp. 517-518.

Cooper Cary L., Philip J., & O Driscoll Michael P., *Organisational Stress: A Review and Critique of Theory Research and Applications*, A Sage Publication Series, New Delhi, 2005, pp. 126-129.

http://www.womenslife.co.za/Default.asp?action=article&ContentID=45

http://stresscourse.tripod.com/id106.html.

http://www.ncbi.nlm.nih.gov/sites/entrez.

3

CHAPTER

Pre-requisites of Self Development *vis-à-vis* Personality

*Rajesh D. Shelke

ABSTRACT

Organizational Behaviour (OB) is the study and application of knowledge about how people, individuals, and groups act in organizations. It does this by taking a system approach. That is, it interprets people-organization relationships in terms of the whole person, whole group, whole organization, and whole social system. Its purpose is to build better relationships by achieving human objectives, organizational objectives, and social objectives. Organization Development (OD) is the systematic application of behavioural science knowledge at various levels, such as group, inter-group, organization, etc., to bring about planned change. The personality of an individual is the total picture of his organised behaviour. Similarly the individual's personality can be described as the analysis pointing out the most important characteristic integration of an individual's structures and activities. There is a need for each individual to improve his personality traits. It is required

* Assistant Professor, Department of Agricultural Economics and Statistics, College of Agriculture, Latur, Marathwada Agricultural University, Parbhani, Maharashtra, India

as each personality has its own strengths and weaknesses, its own limitations. The Multidimensional Assessment of Personality Test (MAP) Test is a psychological instrument that can be administered to senior executives, which gives the score to executives on 20 dimensions. The analysis of MAP test can reveal the strengths and weakness and feedback are provided for self development. A brief description of the 20 primary dimensions measured by MAP is as follows :

Adaptabilities, Achievement, Motivation, Boldness, Competition, Enthusiasm, General ability, Guilt proneness, Imagination, Innovation, Leadership, Maturity, Mental health, Morality, Self control, Sensitivity, Shrewdness, Self sufficiency, Suspiciousness, Social warmth, Tension.

Keywords: Organised behaviour, MAP Test, Dimensions, Personality

Organizational Behavior

So what is organisational behaviour? Put simply, it is the way in which people react to other people and situations in a workplace. A good manager will observe employees so that they are placed in suitable positions within the organisation. If an employee is happy in their position and the situations they have to deal with, they will be more productive. This is not only good for the business but it also gives the employee job satisfaction.

Organizational Behaviour (OB) is the study and application of knowledge about how people, individuals, and groups act in organizations. It does this by taking a system approach. That is, it interprets people-organization relationships in terms of the whole person, whole group, whole organization, and whole social system. Its purpose is to build better relationships by achieving human objectives, organizational objectives, and social objectives.

As you can see from the definition above, organizational behavior encompasses a wide range of topics, such as human behaviour, change, leadership, teams, etc. Since many of these topics are covered elsewhere in the leadership guide, this chapter will focus on a few parts of OB: elements, models, social systems, OD, work life, action learning, and change.

For example, if you had an employee who was a young, shy, softly spoken girl, you would not put her in the role of debt collection. Instead, you might place her in a low stress customer service position that would suit her nature as well as help her to build self-confidence in dealing with customers.

From this, we can see that organisational behaviour is not just about keeping employees happy. It is about putting people in a position that suits their personality and experience as well as helping employees to grow in a way that they become more of an asset to the business.

Aside from recognising the importance of placing employees in positions that will make them happy and productive, you also need to recognise people's reactions to other people. You may have an employee who is quite happy to have you stand behind them, looking over their shoulder while they show you something. Others, however, may feel intimidated or uncomfortable by this, in which case it would be better for you to sit beside them rather than stand over them. If you can't recognise when a person is feeling uncomfortable in a situation, you will find that they will become distracted and thus less productive.

So how do you recognise if someone is uncomfortable in certain situations? Body language! If you are standing too close or if they are uncomfortable with you standing behind them, you will notice that they will move away from you slightly. If you continue to make them uncomfortable, they will most likely pick something up and fiddle with it. You may also find that they will lose their train of thought making it difficult to say whatever it was they were meant to say to you.

These are just some of the basics of organisational behaviour, but as you can see, they can have a huge impact on a person's happiness and productivity in the workplace. Good managers will learn about organisational behaviour to ensure that they can get the most out of their employees and keep them happy at the same time.

Elements of Organizational Behaviour

The organization's base rests on management's philosophy, values, vision and goals. This in turn drives the organizational culture which is composed of the formal organization, informal organization, and the social environment. The culture determines the type of leadership, communication, and group dynamics within the organization. The workers perceive this as the quality of work life which directs their degree of motivation. The final outcomes are performance, individual satisfaction, and personal growth and development. All these elements combine to build the model or framework that the organization operates from.

Models of Organizational Behaviour

There are four major models or frameworks that organizations operate out of:

1. **Autocratic :** The basis of this model is power with a managerial orientation of authority. The employees in turn are oriented towards obedience and dependence on the boss. The employee need that is met is subsistence. The performance result is minimal.
2. **Custodial :** The basis of this model is economic resources with a managerial orientation of money. The employees in turn are oriented towards security and benefits and dependence on the organization. The employee need that is met is security. The performance result is passive cooperation.
3. **Supportive :** The basis of this model is leadership with a managerial orientation of support. The

employees in turn are oriented towards job performance and participation. The employee need that is met is status and recognition. The performance result is awakened drives.

4. **Collegial :** The basis of this model is partnership with a managerial orientation of teamwork. The employees in turn are oriented towards responsible behaviour and self-discipline. The employee need that is met is self-actualization. The performance result is moderate enthusiasm.

Organization Development

Organization Development (OD) is the systematic application of behavioural science knowledge at various levels, such as group, inter-group, organization, etc., to bring about planned change. Its objectives are a higher quality of work-life, productivity, adaptability, and effectiveness. It accomplishes this by changing attitudes, behaviours, values, strategies, procedures, and structures so that the organization can adapt to competitive actions, technological advances, and the fast pace of change within the environment.

There are Seven Characteristics of OD

1. **Humanistic Values:** Positive beliefs about the potential of employees.
2. **Systems Orientation:** All parts of the organization, to include structure, technology, and people, must work together.
3. **Experiential Learning:** The learners' experiences in the training environment should be the kind of human problems they encounter at work. The training should NOT be all theory and lecture.
4. **Problem Solving:** Problems are identified, data is gathered, corrective action is taken, progress is assessed, and adjustments in the problem solving

process are made as needed. This process is known as Action Research.

5. **Contingency Orientation:** Actions are selected and adapted to fit the need.
6. **Change Agent:** Stimulate, facilitate, and coordinate change.
7. **Levels of Interventions:** Problems can occur at one or more level in the organization so the strategy will require one or more interventions.

Organisational Commitment

Many organisations are facing major challenges resulting in restructuring, reengineering and downsizing. The need for factors that predict organisational commitment has become more critical. One of the factors that could lead to healthy organisational climate, increased morale, motivation and productivity organisational commitment. Organisational commitment has emerged as a promising area of research within the study of industrial/organisational psychology in recent time. Organisational commitment was defined as psychological state that binds the individual to the organisation. Organisational commitment is a psychological state that characterizes the employee's relationship with the organisation with its implications for the decision to continue membership in the organisation.

In the following chapter we are concentrating and discussed on one of the major qualities of humans required in the organisational behaviour, organisational development, organisational commitment which is personality.

Personality

The term personality is derived from the latin word 'persona' which means 'mask'. The personality of an individual is the total picture of his organised behaviour. Similarly the individual's personality can be described as the analysis pointing out the most important characteristic integration of an individual's structures and activities. It is a characteristic in a dual sense because

1. it is unique ,this being differentiating element in the individual from all others; and
2. it is fairly consistent.

Personality is a Universal Phenomenon

Personality is a universal phenomenon found only in individual forms. Its pattern is unique. Individuals are commonly described as belonging to certain types. One individual may be said to be ambitious type, another may be conservative and still other may be aggressive.

Personality Pattern

The personality pattern is composed of traits which are organised and integrated into a pattern in which the concept of self is the core. The core of personality pattern is made up of beliefs and attitudes toward self.

Following are the three major factors which are at work in determining the development of personality pattern.

1. The individuals heredity endowment
2. Early experience in the family
3. Important events outside the family environments.

So the personality pattern is not the product of learning or of heredity, but it comes from an interaction of the two.

To Study the Personality

To study the personality of a subject, Thematic Apperception Test can be used with success. TAT is a projective test of personality. The TAT purports to reveal some of the dominant drives, emotions, sentiments, complexes and conflicts of a personality. Following attitudes or traits may be traced in the TAT tests.

- **Abasement :** To a limit—to restraint in order to avoid blame or punishment.

- **Achievement :** To work at something with persistence and to strive to accomplish something creditable in the organisation.
- **Aggression :** To hate to get angry, to quarrel, to blame and to initiate a fight are the states of aggression.
- **Dominance :** To influence others to lead, to mange, to govern are the states of dominance.
- **Nurturance :** To express sympathy to be kind and considerate, to help, to protect are the states of nurturance.
- **Conflict :** A state of uncertainty .An opposition between impulses, desires, needs and aims.
- **Affiliation :** To have friends, to be members of a club are the states of affiliation.

Methods of Observation of Personality

- **Subjective methods :** In this method the subject himself discloses what he knows about himself. He makes himself an object of observation and reports his findings to psychologist.
- **Objective methods :** These appraise the subject is behaviour with the help of a an examiner or judge.
- **Projective methods :** The projective methods of appraising personality differ from both the subjective and the objective by approaching personality indirectly.

Personality Types

The concept of personality types assumes :

- That personality characteristics are mutually exclusive; and
- That in each type is certain mutually dependent and inters-related traits and pattern of response that can be inferred from each other.

There are three types of personality viz.

- Humorous types
- Physical types
- Psychological types

Key inputs of personality

- Executive image
- Appearance
- Communication
- Etiquette
- Behaviour
- Attitude

Structure of Personality

According to Freud the personality consists of id, ego and superego. The id is a reservoir of psychic energy and the source of the human instincts. It provides the power that sustains person's attitudes. The ego is a special part of the id which keeps the individual in touch with the outside world, and finds outlets for the expression of his instinct. The superego is a kind of moral censor which passes judgment on the individual's strivings according to the standards which he has acquired from the parents. It makes him guilty when he goes against those standards, and proud of himself when he lives up to them.

Function of Personality

The individual self has four basic functions which should be present in every individual of the industry. These are thought, feeling, sensation and intuition. Thoughts seek to understand the problems, feelings apprehend it on the basis of a pleasant, unpleasant evaluation, sensations perceive things through the senses and intuition perceives them through an inner awareness.

In addition to these four functions the personality reveals two attitudes .They are introversion and extroversion. The introvert is influenced by what he finds within himself. The extroverts take his bearings from what lies outside himself.

The Assessment of Personality

There are several ways to discover what sort of a personality one has like employing tests, observation of behaviour interviews, questionnaires, rating scales and so on. It would be out of place to discuss them all here, instead we shall deal with a method which is one of the latest and best. This projective method consists of presenting the subject with an ill-defined or unstructured situation which he is asked to interpret in accordance with his own fantasy. This principal has in fact, been found to give insight into the hidden depths of the mind.

Common Qualities of Successful Personalities

If we analyse the personalities of the successful we find that following two qualities are common 1. Persistence and 2. Confidence. Let us examine these two traits in greater detail.

1. **Persistence :** It is an attitude one displays that one's work is meaningful. Persistence can come, however from staying in the job but changing one's attitudes towards it. To stand back, as it were reappraising one's work and finding a new source of interest in it can lead to progress without moving to a new job.
2. **Confidence :** The lack of confidence is one of the principal factors contributing to lack of success. The person who lacks self confidence believes that he is afraid of other people. What he is really afraid of however is his hostility towards other people.

How to Improve Personality

It is very important that we should be able to use our personal assets, potential and traits. Following are some guidelines for improving the personality:

1. Concentrate one thing at a time;
2. Understanding how you came to be, what you are;
3. Imagine oneself, becoming what one wants to be;
4. Guide one's self.

Multi-dimensional Assessment of Personality Test

There is a need for each individual to improve his personality traits. It is required as each personality has its own strengths and weaknesses, its own limitations. The Multi-dimensional Assessment of Personality Test (MAP) Test is a psychological instrument that can be administered to senior executives, which gives the score to executives on 20 dimensions. The analysis of MAP test can reveal the strengths and weakness and feedback is provided for self development. A brief description of the 20 primary dimensions measured by MAP is as follows :

Adaptabilities, Achievement, Motivation, Boldness, Competition, Enthusiasm, General ability, Guilt proneness, Imagination, Innovation, Leadership, Maturity, Mental health, Morality, Self control, Sensitivity, Shrewdness, Self-sufficiency, Suspiciousness, Social warmth and Tension.

Simple combinations of these 20 primary dimensions yields additional dimensions called 'specific skills' and 'supporting factors' such as general ability, leadership, quality, need for achievement, emotional maturity, marketing skills, independence, social skills, stress tolerance and general adjustment. A combination of all these yields a 'Total Personality Score' to give us an exact position of the executives in the group.

References

Hatch, M.J., *"Organization Theory: Modern, Symbolic, and Post-Modern Perspectives."* 2nd Ed. Oxford University Press (2006).

Robbins, Stephen P. *Organizational Behaviour—Concepts, Controversies, Applications.* 4th Ed. Prentice Hall (2004).

Simon, Herbert A. *Administrative Behaviour: A Study of Decision-Making Processes in Administrative Organizations, 4th ed. 1997, The Free Press.*

Tompkins, Jonathan R. "Organization Theory and Public Management". Thompson Wadsworth (2005).

Argyris, C.; Schon, D. (1978), *Organizational Learning: A Theory of Action Perspective,* Reading MA: Addison-Wesley.

Rother, Mike (2009), *Toyota Kata,* McGraw-Hill.

Wendell L French; Cecil Bell. *Organization Development: Behavioural Science Interventions for Organization Improvement.* Englewood Cliffs, N.J.: Prentice-Hall.

Bradford, D.L. & Burke, W.W. eds, (2005). *Organization Development.* San Francisco: Pfeiffer.

Bradford, D.L. & Burke, W.W.(eds), 2005, Reinventing Organization Development. San Francisco: Pfeiffer.

A Study of Manager and Employees' Relationship, Cultural Values and Identity Conflict Management

*Dr. Chimun Kumar Nath

ABSTRACT

As social identity conflicts based on ethnic origin, religion, caste, and so on, erupt around the globe, this chapter investigate what may happen when these conflicts carry over into the workplace. In this chapter an attempt has been made to explore possible employee responses to an organizational manager when the manager is attempting to prevent or reduce the intensity of social identity conflict in the workplace and the conflict is attributed to relatively non-fluid characteristics of social identity such as ethnicity, nationality, caste, or gender. The study proposes that employee responses to manager influence depend on: (1) whether the employee and manager are members of the same or different social identity groups; (2) whether the employees are members of the dominant or non-dominant group in the society at large; and (3) the shared influence of the embedded–autonomous cultural dimensions and the hierarchical–egalitarian cultural dimensions.

Key Words : • cultural values • manager influence • social identity

* Lecturer, Department of Commerce, Dibrugarh University, Dibrugarh, Assam-786004

Prologue

Increasingly, members of non-dominant social identity groups are entering the workplace as employees. This shift in the demographics of the workforce is occurring as an outgrowth of a variety of factors including immigration, political disruption, enfranchisement, globalization, and the need for workers in low birth-rate countries. In many countries, these employees are members of social identity groups who are in conflict with dominant group members in the society at large. Examples of this phenomenon include Moslems and guest workers in Europe, blacks in post-apartheid South Africa, Hispanic immigrants in the US, and Malaysians in Singapore.

In this chapter, the present researcher explores employee responses to a manager who is responsible for preventing or reducing the intensity of social identity conflict in the workplace. In particular, the present researcher is interested in conflicts attributed to differences between social identity groups, such as ethnicity, religion, nationality, caste, or gender, where group membership is relatively fixed and stable. This chapter will add to the existing literature on social identity conflict by examining the interactive effects of a number of variables on employee responses toward manager attempts to address identity-based conflicts. The chapter investigate the circumstances in which managers are likely to be successful in preventing or resolving identity-based conflict, and the circumstances in which employees are likely to ignore or reject a manager's efforts. The present researcher proposes that employee responses to manager influence depend on: (1) whether the employee and manager are members of the same or different social identity groups; (2) whether the employee and the manager are members of the dominant or non-dominant social identity group in the society at large; and (3) the shared influence of the embedded–autonomous cultural dimensions and the hierarchical–egalitarian cultural dimensions.

To develop these propositions an attempt has been made to review and integrate three literatures: social identity theory, social identity leadership theory, and cultural values. The chapter begins with a discussion of the problem of social identity conflict in the workplace and a brief review of the literature that addresses the dynamics of social identity group membership and intergroup conflict. After that the present researcher presents the social identity theory of leadership with particular emphasis on the dynamics that may emerge when the manager and employee represent different social identity groups under conditions of heightened group salience, illustrating these dynamics through the use of interview data. Finally, the chapter introduces cultural values theory and develops propositions to suggest how cultural values may interact with employee and manager identity to predict employee responses to a manager's efforts to resolve identity based conflict.

The Dynamics of Identity Group Membership and the Threat of Group Conflict

Many scholars have written about the human need to identify with social groups in order to feel a sense of belonging as well as to determine their unique place in society. Tajfel (1981: 255) defines social identity as 'that part of an individual's self-concept which derives from his knowledge of his membership of a social group . . . together with the value and emotional significance attached to that membership'. Hogg (2001b: 329) argues that group membership 'renders existence meaningful and thus gives one confidence in how to behave and what to expect from one's physical and social environment'. Brewer (2001: 17) suggests that attachment to ingroups is a primary process, fundamental to individual survival and well-being.

Group membership appears to be important even when the group is of low status in a society. Brewer (2001) distinguishes between group membership and group identification—so one may be a group member, for example a woman, an African-American, a Jew, a Tsutsi, without having a strong identification to that group. On the other hand, Deaux and Martin (2003) demonstrate that group identification is to some degree determined by the perceived alternatives and the permeability of group boundaries. Additionally, one may be treated as a member of a given group by others in accord with societal norms, customs, and history, regardless of one's personal level of identification. Therefore, members of low status non-dominant groups may strongly identify with the group for reasons of survival, differentiation, and uncertainty reduction even if group identification does not bring about enhanced status or self-esteem.

Positive bias toward one's own group is a well-established phenomenon (Brown, 2000) and when one's group is threatened, this positive bias can evolve into dislike and even hate towards members of other groups (Brewer, 2001). Under threat conditions, groups perceive members of other groups as more homogeneous with one another, and polarization may occur where group members develop more extreme positions and less tolerance for deviance within their own groups (Brown, 2000).

The social identity groups of interest in this chapter — group identity based on nationality, gender, religion, ethnicity, caste, and so on — have established histories of conflict in society at large. When employees enter the workforce suspicious and distrustful of other group members, any action by a supervisor, manager, or another employee that is interpreted as a threat to the boundaries of the group, the esteem of the group, the safety of the group, or the certainty of the group's world-view, may trigger group conflict in the workplace. Hogg (2001a: 188) suggests that attributing another person's behaviour to their membership in a social group is 'a fast and relatively automatic cognitive perceptual iterative process that stabilizes when fit is optimized'. In other words, being treated badly by certain 'others' is what members of particular social identity groups have come to expect.

The presence of these groups in the workplace and their changing roles creates the potential for disruptive conflict based on what is known as intergroup anxiety (Stephan and Stephan, 1985). Stephan and Stephan (1985) suggest that intergroup anxiety is created by three sets of factors: prior intergroup relations (e.g. the amount and conditions of prior contact), prior intergroup cognition (e.g. knowledge of the out-group, stereotypes, prejudice, expectations, and perceptions of dissimilarity), and situational factors that characterize the intergroup interaction (e.g. amount of structure, type of interdependence, group composition, relative status).

Intergroup anxiety stems from the anticipation of negative consequences or comparisons as a result of having been in contact with the other group (Fisher, 1990; Stephan and Stephan, 1985). Consequences of intergroup anxiety may include avoidance of intergroup interaction, information processing biases (e.g. seeking information to confirm existing stereotypes), and perceived threat to self-esteem, all of which may increase the likelihood of identity-based conflict (Stephan and Stephan, 1985). Intergroup anxiety heightens the salience of a given social identity and serves as a primer for conflict within the organization.

When social identity conflict threatens to erupt in the workplace, supervisors and managers who hold positions of authority in the organization are usually expected to do something about it (Smith et al., 1998). Social identity theories of leadership suggest that supervisors and managers may find it difficult to fulfill this obligation.

Social Identity Theories of Leadership

Naturally, a manager whose job is to prevent or reduce social identity conflict in the workplace cannot be a member of both groups—for example, Christian and Moslem; native-born and immigrant; male and female. Social identity theories of leadership shed some light on the problems that a manager in this situation is likely to face. Social identity theorists (Haslam, 2001; Hogg, 2001a) posit that the leader of a social identity group will be the person who is most prototypical of that group. In other words, the group member who most represents the ideals and essence of the group is perceived to be the leader and has influence over others because he or she embodies the behaviours to which other group members conform (Hogg et al., 1998). This emerging theory of leadership is unique in that it allows us to predict the extent to which managers will have influence over followers in an intergroup context (Ellemers et al., 2004).

Historically, individual-based theories of leadership would predict that an individual with superior intelligence or task competence would emerge as the group's manager. However, in an intergroup context, group members may gain influence over followers and emerge as leaders for other reasons. For example Turner and Haslam (2001) found that when the leader of a competing group excelled in intelligence, followers of the second group tended to endorse a leader who was unintelligent but considerate, presumably to help distinguish between the two groups. Thus leader prototypicality is context dependent and varies based on the intergroup dynamics involved. Ellemers et al. (2004: 468), state that 'it is not the desirability of the leader's behaviour per se that determines acceptance by his or her followers but the extent to which the behaviour of the manager represents the distinct meaning of their shared identity compared to other groups in that situation'.

Hogg and Reid (2001) propose several social cognitive processes that may explain leadership dynamics. First, self-categorization occurs when group members identify themselves in terms of the defining features of a common and distinctive in-group. Second, depersonalization occurs when proto-typicality rather than individuality becomes the focus of attention, and group members assimilate themselves to the prototype as well as perceive others as out-group members, or nonconforming to the prototype. In terms of intergroup relations, 'the depersonalization process perceptually differentiates groups, and renders perceptions, attitudes, feelings, and behaviors stereotypical and group normative' (Hogg and Reid, 2001: 163).

As a result of such group polarization and salient in-group/out-group boundaries, leaders who best embody a shared group identity will likely emerge as having strong influence over group members. Hogg (2001a: 189–90) argues:

When group membership is salient, people who are perceived to occupy the most prototypical position in the group are perceived to best embody the behaviours to which other, less prototypical members are conforming . . . the most prototypical person appears to exercise the most influence in the group.

Hogg goes on to suggest that social liking will be greater for more prototypical members, giving them greater influence over others. Finally he suggests that this more prototypical group member will be more likely to demonstrate in-group favoritism and intra-group fairness. In terms of this study, it has been interpreted the Hogg's work to mean that when social identity is salient in the work context, the social identity of the organizational manager becomes increasingly important. In fact, Hains et al. (1997) provide empirical support for this notion that, under conditions in which group membership is made salient, perceived manager effectiveness is more strongly related to the group proto-typicality of the manager.

Therefore it can be surmised that under threat conditions (e.g. perceived favouritism, insult, disrespect, inequity, etc.), employees who do not share social identity group membership characteristics with the manager who is attempting to intervene in a conflict will reject the manager's efforts, and group polarization will increase.

Proposition 1: When the manager is from the same social identity group as the followers, he or she is perceived as a more prototypical member of the group, and therefore is allowed to exert more power and influence in resolving identity-based conflicts.

Ellemers et al.'s (2004) work suggests that followers will be more inclined to hold positive expectations about the motives and intentions of their managers when they are perceived as in-group members than when they are perceived to be out-group members.

They state that, 'the potential of leaders to communicate and create a sense of shared identity is an important determinant of the likelihood that their attempts to energize, direct, and sustain particular work-related behaviours in their followers will be successful' (2004: 467). Therefore it can be concluded that when managers are not perceived as in-group members, they will have difficulty creating a shared identity and may subsequently struggle to motivate and guide group performance, especially in conflict situations.

Hogg and Terry (2000) offer two actions that an organizational manager might employ to try to alter the employee's perception of the manager's social identity when there is a manager/follower identity mismatch. The manager may try to emphasize another aspect of his or her social identity—for example, his role as an expert or as a member of a shared professional group. The manager may also try to focus on the task and emphasize her task competence. Brewer and Miller's work (1984) suggests that managers may be more effective if their contacts with employees are person based rather than category based, however Brewer and Brown (1998) caution that while personalization may alter in-group stereotypes, it does not always reduce prejudice, because positive interpersonal experiences do not necessarily generalize to attitudes toward a whole group. Regardless of the approach, when demographic group membership is salient, these strategies will be difficult to employ and Hogg and Terry address this situation.

In their article on social identity and self categorization in organizations, Hogg and Terry (2000: 127; emphasis added) write:

> If relations between demographic groups are conflictual and emotionally charged [*in the society at large*] diversity will highlight intergroup relations outside the organization, thus making demographic membership salient and strengthening adherence to demographic – not organizational—norms.

In the next section two examples of the dynamic of employee/manager identity mismatch under conditions of heightened identity group salience has been highlighted. These examples were selected from a dataset of confidential interviews conducted by the author in a pilot study of leadership and social identity conflict in the workplace. The first example, taken from an organization in Assam, provides three observations describing a manager's style. The first two quotes illustrate a manager/employee match. The employees and the manager are Bengali and the Bengali employees are discussing whether or not this manager treats Bengali employees better than Assamese employees. The third quote illustrates a mismatch and is from an Assamese employee discussing the same issue. It is important to note that there is a history of Linguistic tension in this organization. As part of an effort for senior management to demonstrate fairness, a Bengali male has been appointed to a team manager role.

Organization 1

The first quote is from a Bengali male speaking about his Bengali supervisor:

> "He's not hard on them [the Assamese employees] but they sit there and cry if you ask them to do something

over and beyond. Sometimes they won't do anything. They'll do it but they'll feel like the man is picking on them . . . I know you've heard all this, that the work manager is lenient on certain people. He's not lenient. Nine times out of ten, if you've done your job, he ain't going to bother you. He's like this. He's got a loud bark. If you don't know him, you don't know if he's joking or not. But if you're lazy, he's going to stick on you. He will stay on you."

The next quote is from a second Bengali male speaking about this supervisor:

"He's just a very stern person. He's stern; stand up. He just tells you what is on his mind. If he feels like you're not doing your job, he'll tell you, you need to do your job. Does he play favorites at all? That's a rumour in the shop. I haven't seen it. We work together. We don't hang out after work or anything like that. But if I'm not pulling my load, he gets on me just like I've seen him get on other guys . . . But most people don't see him as stern. They just see him as a mean type person. Until you get to know him, he don't smile all the time. He's very work oriented. I guess that's the way to put it."

And the third quote is from an Assamese male speaking of this Bengali supervisor:

"There was an individual who is non-Assamese and it has been alleged on several occasions that he is very prejudiced. In the past I have seen certain—I don't want to go so far as to say favouritism—but I have seen things happen with non-Assamese groups in his department that don't happen with Assamese. I honestly feel that the Assamese male is fast becoming extinct, not necessarily in the workplace but in the entire society."

In these three quotes, the salience of linguistic group membership is apparent, as well as the fact that attributions of manager behaviour seem to be drawn along historically linguistic lines. Bengalis attribute the behaviour of the Bengali supervisor to his being stern or work-oriented, while Assamese attribute his behaviour to favouritism.

This example seems to lend support to the first hypothesis. The Bengali supervisor appears to be conferred with more power and influence by his Bengali employees than his Assamese employee. The second example comes from an employee training programme in Meghalaya where adults from the entire state assemble to receive job skills training. The informant is a Khashi, and the groups in conflict are Khashes and Non-Khashes. The managers are Khasi, Assamese, and Mizo. This example illustrates an employee/ manager mismatch on several levels. According to the informant, there are status differences in the society at large between the various ethnic groups present in this example, as well as a general resentment of outsiders by host state.

Organization 2

This quote is from a Khashi informant speaking about his Assamese peer and a Mizo manager:

> "The conflict centered on an assistant principal of Assamese origin. He had managed to gather a few people around him who were so loyal to him and not necessarily loyal to the organization or the business objectives of the organization, including himself. And that was perceived to be against the interests of the Khashi people who were in the teaching staff. This situation snowballed and resulted in open conflict and the Khashis' didn't have as much authority because they were teaching staff, whereas this man was the assistant principal and I was an assistant principal too at the time, but we had a Mizo principal and the Mizo principal was trying to steer the ship in the right direction, but this Assamese had so much power around him that he simply could not comply with the directions of the company and it created a lot of difficulty for everybody and the result was many of the Sudanese

teachers resigned en masse. So we had about five people coming in and submitting their resignations in one day."

This case illustrates the influence of multiple identities and also the failure of the Mizo or Khashi authority figures to stop the Assamese manager from demonstrating favouritism or prevent the Khashi teachers from resigning. The salience of social identity and the perceptions of favouritism were stronger than the authority structure of the organization.

To summarize, when the workforce is made up of demographically diverse social identity group members who bring with them a history of intergroup tension from society at large, they enter the workplace with at least some degree of discomfort, distrust, or antipathy toward members of other social identity groups. A social identity theory of leadership would predict that when this discomfort or distrust erupts into group tension or conflict, demographic characteristics of the employees and the manager will be heightened, making it difficult for the manager to intervene in the conflict when there is an employee/manager identity mismatch. Social identity theorists have demonstrated that efforts taken by a manager to reduce tension will be judged more favourably by employees who share group membership with the manager on the salient social identity characteristics (e.g. Hogg, 2001a; Hogg and Martin, 2003; Hogg and Terry, 2000).

These two examples illustrate that the amount of power and influence conferred on a manager from the same social identity group is higher than that conferred on a manager from a different social identity group.

The Interaction of Manager/Employee Identity and Cultural Values

As it has been discussed, social identity theory posits that the group leader is perceived to be the most prototypical member of the group. This proto-typicality may be reflected in the appearance, espoused beliefs, or behaviors that group members believe represent the essence of group identification. It has been suggested social identity dynamics will make it more difficult for a manager to prevent or reduce social identity conflict in the organization when the social identity characteristics are fixed, since, by definition, the manager cannot be a member of both groups and intergroup anxiety serves to heighten the salience of social identity group memberships.

However, because the meaning of social identity group membership and the legitimacy of the power accorded a given social identity group will vary based on the cultural context; let us turn to a discussion of cultural values and the interaction between social identity mismatch and cultural dimensions.

Cultures differ from one another along basic dimensions (Hofstede, 1980, 1991, 2001; House et al. 2004; Inglehart, 1997; Schwartz, 1994; Smith et al., 1996), and these cultural dimensions have influence on the policies, procedures, norms and actions of employees in organizations (Dickson et al., 2000; Spony, 2003). In this chapter we use Schwartz's taxonomy as the basis for developing the propositions, although it has been reported the literature from studies using other dimensions as well.

Shalom Schwartz (1994, 1999) proposes seven dimensions of cultural values that: reflect the basic issues or problems that societies must confront in order to regulate human behaviour . . . the nature of the relationship of the individual to the group is defined by the bi-polar dimension, Embeddedness vs. Autonomy; the legitimate distribution of power, roles, and resources is defined by the bi-polar dimension, Hierarchy versus Egalitarianism; and the relationship of humankind to the natural and social world is defined as Mastery versus Harmony. (1999; 24) The definitions are given in Table 4.1.

Table 4.1 Cultural values (Schwartz, 1999)

To what extent are persons autonomous vs. *embedded in their groups?*

Embeddedness — A culture in which the person is viewed as an entity who is embedded in the collectivity and finds meaning in life largely through social relationships, through identifying with the group and participating in its shared way of life.

Autonomous — A culture in which the person is viewed as an autonomous, bounded entity that finds meaning in his or her own uniqueness . . . and is encouraged to do so. Autonomy has two components: intellectual autonomy and affective autonomy.

The guarantee of responsible social behaviour and the preservation of the social fabric

Hierarchy — A cultural emphasis on the legitimacy of an unequal distribution of power, roles and resources

Egalitarianism — A cultural emphasis on transcendence of selfish interest in favour of voluntary commitment to promoting the welfare of others.

The relationship of humankind to the natural and social world

Mastery — A cultural emphasis on getting ahead through active self-assertion, through changing and mastering the natural and social environment.

Harmony — A cultural emphasis on fitting harmoniously into the environment.

Schwartz has demonstrated that a circle provides the best structural relationship for these dimensions, so that values most closely related to one another are in proximity around the circle and contradictory value types are in opposition on the circle. First of all it explores how cultural values that influence the relationship of the individual to the group may interact with social identity match/mismatch between the manager and employee.

The Relationship of the Individual to the Group

The social psychology literature tells us that individuals differ in the strength of their group identification (Deaux and Martin, 2003; Ellemers et al., 1997). This means that in response to group identity threat (e.g. a threat to the group's prestige, its values, its safety, and its symbols), some members will attempt to coalesce with the group, while others will attempt to leave the group and seek more attractive alternatives. Ellemers et al. (1997) demonstrated that low identifiers perceived their group as less homogeneous, were less committed to their group, and were more strongly desirous of individual mobility than high identifiers, regardless of the permeability of the group boundaries and the status of the group.

The literature has also established that the strength of group identification is contingent on culture. In collectivist cultures individuals belong to fewer groups and there is less variability among group members in the strength of group attachment (Brewer, 2001; Triandis, 1995). The person is embedded in the collectivity and finds meaning through social relationships and identification with the group (Schwartz, 1999: 27). The view of self is determined by one's interdependence with others and one's status as a participant in the larger social unit (Markus and Kitayama, 1991).

One consequence of this is that within collectivist cultures, in-group/out-group distinctions are stronger, and the implications of group membership may be seen in cross-group interactions. A number of scholars have determined that when there are in-groups and out-groups within a collectivist culture, members of the in-group are more likely to distrust out-group members (Fukuyama, 1995), be less generous, and behave in a harsh and contentious manner with out-group members, more so than with in-group members (Leung, 1988; Leung and Bond, 1984).

Therefore, if a manager is perceived to be a member of the out-group as a result of his or her social identity group status, then the manager will have difficulty exerting influence over the group. This suggests that in countries where embedded or collectivist values are dominant and group identity is paramount, employee/manager identity differences will be more salient, and employees may be more likely to reject a manager's efforts to intervene in a social identity group conflict when the manager is considered to be a member of the out-group. A manager who fails to fit the prototype for certain group members is more likely to be perceived as an out-group member, and less able to create a shared identity for the workgroup, regardless of any managerial strategy he or she adopts in an attempt to unite the group.

Additionally, a number of scholars in the conflict and culture literature have demonstrated differences in intercultural and intra-cultural conflict styles that may well co-vary with identity group membership and exacerbate in-group/out-group dynamics (e.g. Derlega et al., 2002; Holt and Devore, 2005; Kozan, 1997; Ting-Toomey et al., 1991). For example, Kozan and Ergin (1999) use Schwartz's individual-level values survey to demonstrate that employees of 40 Turkish organizations who valued tradition, security, and conformity were more likely to embrace an avoiding style of conflict management.

These individual-level intra-cultural differences were observed within the context of a country that falls within the embedded dimension on Schwartz's cultural values scale (Schwartz, 2004). This research suggests that a non-prototypical manager (i.e. an out-group member) who uses a conflict management strategy that runs counter to that which is valued in a particular cultural context is likely to exacerbate trust issues, particularly in collectivistic or embedded cultures.

In countries where autonomous or individualistic values are dominant and there is an employee/manager mismatch, employee responses to managerial strategies may be less determined by the social identity of the leader and more determined by the strength of group members' attachment to their own social identity group. In individualistic cultures, the self is perceived as relatively independent of social identity groups, and personal attitudes tend to be more important determinants of organizational behaviours than social identity group norms or values (Gelfand et al., 2004: 446; Markus and Kitayama, 1991). Individuals from autonomous cultures tend to emphasize the independent pursuit of individual ideas, intellectual directions, and affective experiences (Schwartz, 1999). Generally speaking, the importance of social identity group membership is more variable in individualistic or autonomous cultures.

If followers in autonomous/individualistic cultures have a strong identification with their social identity group, then they may reject the leader's efforts because the leader is not perceived as prototypical. However, if followers in autonomous/individualistic cultures have a weak identification with their social identity group, they may be more likely to accept the leader's efforts to resolve identity based conflicts. This leads us to conclude that the social identity of the manager—the manager as the prototypical group member—would be more critical in embedded cultures than in autonomous cultures.

Proposition 2: Social group identity is more salient and group distinctions are stronger in embedded/collectivist cultures. Therefore, manager/employee social identity match will play a more significant role during social identity conflicts that emerge at work in embedded/collectivist cultures than in autonomous/individualist cultures.

The Legitimacy of the Distribution of Power, Roles, Resources, and Status

Other studies have been conducted investigating the influence of the dimensions of culture related to power and role distribution on various organizational practices, although studies on the power distance/hierarchical dimensions of culture are much less numerous or conclusive than those investigating the individual in relationship to the group. In a 1998 study, Smith et al. explored the relationship of espoused values and the handling of disagreement in 23 countries. In this study, high power distance was not found to be related to reliance on superiors to handle disagreements.

Smith et al. (1998) concluded that because organizational roles confer power to superiors in collectivist and individualist cultures, these role prescriptions may override cultural differences. Indeed the mean scores of the countries in this study support the conclusion that superiors play the most critical role in determining how disagreements are handled.

This suggests that in countries that endorse the hierarchical pole of the hierarchy–egalitarianism dimension, managers may actually find it easier to prevent or reduce social identity conflict, regardless of manager/employee identity differences. That is because differences in societal roles that equate to an unequal distribution of power and status reflected in organizational roles would be perceived to be legitimate. In this situation, we might surmise that the manager, most likely a member of the dominant group, would be expected to step in and prevent social identity conflict, and his or her efforts would be accepted by both dominant and non-dominant group members.

Proposition 3: Leaders will exert more influence in resolving social identity conflicts in hierarchical cultures, regardless of their social group identity. This proposition is somewhat contradictory to our second proposition, which suggests that manager/employee social identity match is significant in resolving social identity conflicts. Therefore we suggest that a more satisfactory approach to understanding the influence of culture involves the simultaneous consideration of multiple cultural dimensions; something we elaborate on in the next section.

Interactive Effects of Cultural Values and Manager/Employee Social Identity

The values of a country are complex. Countries are not influenced solely by single dimensions of cultural values, and while only a few studies have been conducted examining the influence of combined cultural dimensions, the approach is theoretically rich. Schwartz (1999: 29) suggests that while value types in opposition to one another on the circle express alternative resolutions to basic human issues ('An emphasis on one value type is postulated to be accompanied in a culture by a de-emphasis on the polar type'), values that are in proximity to one another share similar assumptions. Schwartz suggests that shared cultural influences underpin dimensions that are adjacent to one another in cultural space. For example, hierarchical and embedded cultures both reflect social interdependence and mutual obligation among in-group members: 'Embeddedness and hierarchy share the assumption that a person's roles in and obligations to collectivities are more important than her unique ideas and aspirations' (Schwartz, 2004: 48). If we consider our thesis in terms of shared cultural dimensions, a more satisfactory and perhaps more complete set of propositions emerge.

In cultures characterized as having the values of embeddedness and hierarchy, in-group/out-group distinctions are highly salient, and status and power differences between in-groups and out-groups is expected and perceived as legitimate. Manager/employee identity differences may be more salient to members of the dominant group than to those of the non-dominant group.

When considering employee acceptance of managerial attempts to address social identity conflicts, members of the dominant social identity group might be expected to reject managerial direction from a member of the non-dominant social identity group because acceptance would constitute a double threat–a threat to the group's hegemony, and a threat to the group's esteem. In other words, because the status of dominant group members is legitimized by the hierarchical values, the hegemony of the dominant group must be preserved, and loyalty to the in-group may be enhanced.

From the perspective of the non-dominant group members, however, the legitimacy of role prescriptions in society at large and the organization, as suggested by Smith et al. (1998), may strongly influence superior/subordinate interactions. It can be proposed that members of the non-dominant group may accept managerial direction from a dominant group member — even in the case of social identity mismatch, because of the perceived legitimacy and impermeability of the role relationships within a society, and the legitimacy of the individual's organizational power, regardless of the importance of social identity group membership within an embedded culture.

Proposition 4: When a social identity group mismatches between the employee and manager occurs in embedded/ collectivistic and hierarchical cultures, employees from the non-dominant social identity group will probably accept the efforts of managers from the dominant social identity group to prevent or reduce social identity conflict. However, employees from the dominant social identity group are likely to reject the efforts of managers from the non-dominant social identity group (i.e. autonomous/individualistic and egalitarian), in spite of their position of power within the organization.

Interestingly, Smith et al. (1998: 355) suggest that formal rules and procedures for handling disagreements are preferred in collectivist cultures since they enable disagreements to be handled in an impersonal way, thus preserving in-group harmony. It might be that in the case of disagreements attributed to social identity, when there are salient identity differences between the manager and a subset of employees, it is also better to use formal rules and procedures to handle the disagreement, regardless of cultural context, since this may reduce the salience and impact of social identity group categorization and at the same time protect the esteem and group boundaries of the non-dominant group.

In countries characterized as both autonomous and egalitarian, Schwartz (1999) suggests that the shared cultural influences of these two dimensions incorporate the notion of the autonomous social being—the individual is viewed as an autonomous decision maker who accepts the nature of human relationships as contractual. Schwartz (2004) notes that autonomy and egalitarianism share the assumption that people can and should take individual-level responsibility for their actions, and make decisions based on their own personal understanding of the situation.

Therefore, one would expect the strength of an individual's relationship to the group to dictate the response to a manager's intervention in the case of a manager/ employee identity difference. In other words, the predictions of social identity theories of leadership would hold true: manager/employee social identity mismatch would matter when identity group membership is salient to the individuals involved. However, managers might more easily alter this salience, as group members would be less centrally attached to any single group.

Members of individualistic or autonomous cultures apply equity norms to determine the costs and benefits of social relationships, and rationally consider the impact these relationships will have on their own personal needs and values (Gelfand et al., 2004; Oyserman et al., 2002). Therefore managers may be more likely to exert influence over employees to prevent or reduce social identity conflicts in autonomous/individualistic and egalitarian cultures because social identity group categorization is more fluid and impermanent (Oyserman et al., 2002), and employees may be more likely to shift in-group/out-group boundaries and recognize others in the workplace as moral equals with shared interests (Schwartz, 1999). Therefore, managerial strategies to prevent or resolve social identity conflicts in the workplace may be particularly effective in embedded/individualistic and egalitarian cultures when individual identification with social identity groups is weak and the manager effectively appeals to the employees' desire to cooperate and consider the welfare of all as moral equals.

Proposition 5: In societies where the values of autonomy/individualism and egalitarianism prevail, individual differences in the strength of group identification and the success of managerial attempts to promote cooperation and collective welfare will result in positive employee responses to managerial attempts to prevent or reduce social identity conflict.

Summary and Implications for Research

Social identity group members enter the workforce with a salient social identity based on certain demographic characteristics. The salience of this identity is maintained by contentious historical and contemporary relationships between groups in society at large. It is the responsibility of those who hold managerial roles in organizations to keep this conflict from erupting in the workplace. Social identity theories of leadership suggest that if there is a mismatch between managers and employees on salient aspects of social identity, managers may find it difficult to resolve social identity conflict in the workplace, but that the manager can reduce the perception of mismatch by invoking other identities. It can be argued that the influence of the mismatch on employee acceptance of the manager's efforts must be considered within the context of cultural values. The permeability of group boundaries, the strength of group attachment, and the perceived legitimacy of role relationships between dominant and non-dominant group members will all contribute to the choices available to a manager and the probability of his or her success in reducing social group conflict in the workplace.

There are many variables beyond the scope of this article that most certainly affect an employee's response to a manager's attempts to quell social identity conflict in the workplace. These include, but are not limited to, the nature of the organization (private *vs.* state owned, for profit *vs.* not for profit, national *vs.* international), the type of employee

(White collar *vs.* blue collar), the nature and strength of the organizational culture, and job opportunities within a city or country, to name a few.

The propositions developed in this article are an attempt to reconcile the apparent contradictions that emerge from two important streams of work — social identity theory and cultural values research. These propositions are based on the premise that the successful management of social identity-based conflict in organizations demands an acknowledgement of the context-bound nature of the phenomena. Therefore the testing of these propositions must also be grounded in context.

To avoid the inadvertent imposition of a particular cultural frame onto the outcomes it can be suggested that an ethnographic and grounded theory strategy of design and analysis be employed. The components of such an approach might include interviews developed by an international team in the language of the interviewee, and conducted by in-country researchers with employees representing different organizational levels and social identity groups within different types of organizations (for profit, not for profit, multinational, national, manufacturing, service).

Additionally organizations would be selected from places that vary significantly on cultural value dimensions. The analysis of these interviews would be conducted and analysed by an in-place team, while the comparison of themes between and across places would be conducted by an international research team. Although such an approach is time-consuming and expensive — less efficient than the simple administration of surveys — it is more likely to produce a true understanding of the phenomenon. This approach may best prevent what Kuo-Shu Yang describes as 'the artificiality, superficiality, and incompatibility' (2004: 16) that result from applying western psychology to local cultures. Rather, holding these propositions as a loose framework, local interviewers may study the phenomenon in the country before addressing the phenomenon at the cross cultural level.

References

Brewer, M.B. (2001) 'Ingroup Identification and Intergroup Conflict', in R.D. Ashmore, L. Jussim and D. Wilder (eds) *Social Identity, Intergroup Conflict, and Conflict Reduction*, pp. 17–41. Oxford: Oxford University Press.

Brewer, M.B. and Brown, R.J. (1998) 'Intergroup Relations', in D.T. Gilbert, S.T. Fiske and G. Lindzey (eds) *The Handbook of Social Psychology*, Vol. 2, 4th edn, pp. 554–95. New York: McGraw-Hill.

Brewer, M.B. and Miller, N. (1984) 'Beyond the Contact Hypothesis: Theoretical Perspectives on Desegregation', in N. Miller and M.B. Brewer (eds) *Groups in Contact: The Psychology of Desegregation*, pp. 281–302. New York: Academic Press.

Brown, R. (2000) 'Social Identity Theory: Past Achievements, Current Problems and Future Challenges', *European Journal of Social Psychology* 30: 745–78.

Deaux, K. and Martin, D. (2003) 'Interpersonal Networks and Social Categories: Specifying Levels of Context in Identity Processes', *Social Psychology Quarterly* 66: 101–17.

Derlega, V.J., Cukur, C.S., Kuang, J.C.Y. and Forsyth, D.R. (2002) 'Interdependent Construal of Self and the Endorsement of Conflict Resolution Strategies in Interpersonal, Intergroup, and International Disputes', *Journal of Cross-Cultural Psychology* 33(6): 610–25.

Dickson, M., Aditya, R. and Chokar, J. (2000) 'Definitions and Interpretations in Crosscultural Organizational Culture Research: Some Pointers from the GLOBE Research Program', in N. Ashkanasy, C. Wilderom and M. Peterson (eds) *Handbook of Organizational Culture and Climate*. Thousand Oaks, CA: Sage.

Ellemers, N., de Gilder, D. and Haslam, S. (2004) 'Motivating Individuals and Groups at Work: A Social Identity Perspective on Leadership and Group Performance', *Academy of Management Review* 29: 459–78.

Ellemers, N., Spears, R. and Doosje, B. (1997) 'Sticking Together or Falling Apart: In-group Identification as a Psychological Determinant of Group Commitment *versus* Individual Mobility', *Journal of Personality and Social Psychology* 72(3): 617–26.

Fisher, R.J. (1990) 'Needs Theory, Social Identity and an Eclectic Model of Conflict', in J. Burton (ed.) *Conflict: Human Needs Theory*. New York: St Martin's Press.

Fukuyama, F. (1995) *Trust: The Social Virtues and the Creation of Prosperity*. New York: Free Press.

Gelfand, M.J., Bhawuk, D.P.S., Nishi, L.H. and Bechtold, D.J. (2004) 'Individualism and Collectivism', in R.J. House, P.J. Hanges, M. Javidan, P.W. Dorfman and V. Gupta (eds) *Culture, Leadership, and Organizations* (pp. 437–512). Thousand Oaks, CA: Sage.

Hains, S.G., Hogg, M.A. and Duck, J.M. (1997) 'Self-categorization and Leadership: Effects of Group Prototypicality and Manager Stereotypicality', *Personality and Social Psychology Bulletin*, 23(10): 1087–99.

Haslam, S.A. (2001) *Psychology in Organizations: The Social Identity Approach*. London: Sage.

Hofstede, G. (1980) *Culture's Consequences: International Differences in Work-related Values*. Beverly Hills, CA: Sage.

Hofstede, G. (1991) *Cultures and Organizations: Software of the Mind*. London: McGraw-Hill.

Hofstede, G. (2001) *Culture's Consequences: Comparing Values, Behaviours, Institutions, and Organizations across Nations*. Thousand Oaks, CA: Sage.

Hogg, M.A. (2001a) 'A Social Identity Theory of Leadership', *Personality and Social Psychology Review* 5(3): 184–200.

Hogg, M.A. (2001b) 'Self-categorization and Subjective Uncertainty Resolution: Cognitive and Motivational Facets of Social Identity and Group Membership', in J.P. Forgas, K.D. Williams and L. Wheeler (eds) *The Social Mind: Cognitive and Motivational Aspects of Interpersonal Behaviour*, pp. 323–49. Cambridge: Cambridge University Press.

Hogg, M.A. and Martin, R. (2003) 'Social Identity Analysis of Manager–Member Relations: Reconciling Self-categorization and Manager–Member Exchange Theories of Leadership', in S.A. Haslam, D. Van Knippenberg, M.J. Platow and N. Ellemers (eds) *Social Identity at Work: Developing Theory for Organizational Practice*, pp. 139–54. New York: Psychology Press.

Hogg, M.A. and Reid, S.A. (2001) 'Social Identity, Leadership, and Power', in A.Y. Lee-Chai and J.A. Bargh (eds) *The Use and Abuse of Power: Multiple Perspectives on the Causes of Corruption*, pp. 159–80. New York: Psychology Press.

Hogg, M.A. and Terry, D.J. (2000) 'Social Identity and Self-categorization Processes in Organizational Contexts', *Academy of Management Review* 25: 121–40.

Hogg, M.A., Hains, S.C. and Mason, I. (1998) 'Identification and Leadership in Small Groups: Salience, Frame of Reference, and Manager Stereotypicality Effects on Manager Evaluations', *Journal of Personality and Social Psychology* 75(5): 1248–63.

Holt, J.L. and DeVore, C.J. (2005) 'Culture, Gender, Organizational Role, and Styles of Conflict Resolution: A Meta-analysis', *International Journal of Intercultural Relations* 29: 165–96.

House, R.J., Hanges, P.J., Javidan, M., Dorfman, P.W., Gupta, V. and GLOBE Associates (eds) (2004) *Cultures, Leadership and Organizations: Project GLOBE – A 62 Nation Study*, Vol. 1. Thousand Oaks, CA: Sage.

Inglehart, R. (1997) *Modernization and Post Modernization: Cultural, Economic, and Political Change in 43 Societies.* Princeton, NJ: Princeton University Press.

Kozan, M.K. (1997) 'The Influence of Intracultural Value Difference on Conflict Management Practices', *The International Journal of Conflict Management* 8(4): 338–60.

Kozan, M.K. and Ergin, C. (1999) 'The Influence of Intra-cultural Value Differences on Conflict Management Practices', *The International Journal of Conflict Management* 10(3):249–67.

Kuo-Shu Yang (2004) 'Indigenous Psychology, Westernized Psychology, and Indigenized Psychology: A Non-western Psychologist's View', in G. Zheng, J. Ren and L. Hua (eds) *Proceedings from the XVII International Congress for Cross-Cultural Psychology*, pp.16–17. Xi'an, China.

Leung, K. (1988) 'Some Determinants of Conflict Avoidance', *Journal of Cross Cultural Psychology* 19: 125–36.

Leung, K. and Bond, M.H. (1984) 'The Impact of Cultural Collectivism on Reward Allocation', *Journal of Personality and Social Psychology* 4: 793–804.

Markus, H.R. and Kitayama, S. (1991) 'Culture and the Self: Implications for Cognition, Emotion, and Motivation', *Psychological Review* 98(2): 224–53.

Oyserman, D., Coon, H.M. and Kemmelmeier, M. (2002) 'Rethinking Individualism and Collectivism: Evaluation of Theoretical Assumptions and Meta-analyses', *Psychological Bulletin* 128: 3–72.

Schwartz, S.H. (1994) 'Beyond Individualism/Collectivism, New Cultural Dimensions of Values', in U. Kim, H.C. Triandis, C. Kagitcibasi, S.C. Choi and G. Yoon (eds) *Individualism and Collectivism: Theory, Methods, and Applications*, pp. 85–119. Beverly Hills, CA: Sage.

Schwartz, S.H. (1999) 'A Theory of Cultural Values and Some Implications for Work', *Applied Psychology: An International Review* 48(1):23–47.

Schwartz, S.H. (2004) 'Mapping and Interpreting Cultural Differences Around the World', in H. Vinken, J. Soeters and P. Ester (eds) *Comparing Cultures, Dimensions of Culture in a Comparative Perspective*, pp.43–73. Leiden, The Netherlands: Brill.

Smith, P.B., Dugan, S. and Trompenaars, F. (1996) 'National Culture and Managerial Values: A Dimensional Analysis Across 43 Nations', *Journal of Cross Cultural Psychology* 27: 252–85.

Smith, P.B., Peterson, M.F., Leung, K. and Dugan, S. (1998) 'Individualism–Collectivism and the Handling of Disagreement: A 23 Country Study', *International Journal of Intercultural Relations* 22: 351–67.

Spony, G. (2003) 'The Development of a Work-value Model Assessing the Cumulative Impact of Individual and Cultural Differences on Managers' Work-value Systems: Empirical Evidence from French and British Managers', *International Journal of Human Resource Management* 14(4): 658–97.

Stephan, W.G. and Stephan, C.W. (1985) 'Intergroup Anxiety', *Journal of Social Issues* 41: 157–75.

Tajfel, H. (1981) *Human Groups and Social Categories.* Cambridge: Cambridge University Press.

Ting-Toomey, S., Geo, G., Trubisky, P., Yang, Z., Kim, H.S., Lin, S. and Nishida, T. (1991)

'Culture, Face Maintenance, and Styles of Handling Interpersonal Conflict: An Updated Face-negotiation Theory', *International Journal of Intercultural Relations* 22: 187–225.

Triandis, H.C. (1995) *Individualism and Collectivism*. Boulder, CO: Westview Press.

Turner, J.C. and Haslam, S.A. (2001) 'Social Identity, Organizations, and Leadership', in J.C. Turner (ed.) *Groups at Work: Theory and Research*, pp. 25–65. Mahwah, NJ: Lawrence Erlbaum Associates.

CHAPTER

Participatory Communication for Sustainable Development

An Organized Management Approach

*Dr. Mahendra Kumar Padhy

ABSTRACT

In this chapter, an attempt has been made to identify and delineate the role of participatory management communication in general and specific roles of various communication channels in meeting the goals of sustainable development in particular. In case of specificity, the manner in which participatory communication plays its role for sustainable development is discussed in detail. Sustainable development is an integrated and holistic approach that calls for the participation of individuals, groups, organizations (particularly the NGO's), public and governments at local, regional, national and global levels. The goal of sustainable development is not confined to one locality or region or nation but embraces the entire globe. It extends not for a few years, but for the distant future too. Thus spatially or temporally its scope is very wide. It requires people to think globally and act locally for the development and growth of rural sectors.

* Presently working as an Associate Professor in the Department of Mass Communication and Journalism, School of Information Science and Technology, Babasaheb Bhimrao Ambedkar University (A Central University), Vidya Vihar, Lucknow, U.P.-226 025

Informed and conscious citizens can utilize poverty alleviation programmes effectively and successfully. Informed and conscious citizens can also play a responsible role in promoting environmental protection in various walks of their lives.. In fact to fulfill the goals of sustainable development there is an indispensable need to mould a lifestyle that is environment friendly and equitable all over the world.

Communication management in general and various communication channels in particular have a potential role to play in moulding such a lifestyle. Poverty eradication, protecting the environment, reducing the consumption of non-renewable resources and increasing the use of renewable resources, conservation of biological diversity, land degradation and deforestation, waste management, using appropriate technologies, land reforms, population control and stabilization, upholding basic human rights, social welfare and women's upliftment, promoting intra-generational and inter-generational equity, and participation of people from individual, local levels to global levels, being the various important objectives of sustainable development, different communication channels have a potential role to play in fulfilling these objectives. Though communication alone is not sufficient to meet these objectives, it is a crucial element in facilitating the fulfillment of these objectives.

Key Words : • cultural values • manager influence • social identity

Introduction

The concept of sustainable development has occupied a central place in every aspect of human life today. It is a multidimensional and multidisciplinary concept covering almost all spheres of human activity. Sustainable development has become the concern of economists, ecologists, administrators, lawyers, communication experts, environmentalists, human right activists, feminists, scientists and NGO's. In other words, it has become everybody's cup of tea. Since the present study aims at studying the role of communication in sustainable development without identifying the various implications of the concept. Therefore, an attempt has been made in this chapter to discuss the various implications of sustainable development.

The World Commission on Environment and Development (WCED, 1987) defined "sustainable development as the development that meets the needs of the present without compromising the ability of future generations to meet their own needs."

It is observed that sustainable development is a coin which consists of two obligations on its two sides. One side is the alleviation of poverty and the other, the protection of environment. Sustainable development is very much linked with the involvement and active participation of people. It is a holistic concept that can be on the global, national, local and individual scale. Communication is an intervening variable without which the materialization of different goals of sustainable development is not possible. Therefore. Communication has the key role in facilitating the participation of people relating to sustainable development.

Conceptual Framework

The present study has been taken up with the following theoretical framework. There are a myriad of theories and models of communication, but there are only a few theories and models which deal with the questions of development. Therefore it is useful to discuss the relevant models and theories in the context of the present study as follows.

Development media theory deals with the task of media in developing countries. It emphasizes the positive uses of the media in national development and for the autonomy and society. To a certain extent elements of this theory favour democratic and grassroots involvement, thus promoting participative communication models. (Mcquail,1987) The one thing of the media is the acceptance of economic development itself and often the correlated nation building, as an overriding objective. To this end, certain freedom of the media and of journalists is subordinated to their responsibility of helping in this purpose. Collective ends rather than individual freedoms are emphasized.

With the failure of the Dominant Paradigm of development, and its communication approach in bringing about the expected change, there took place a thinking about the alternative paradigm of development which led to the emergence of the concept of another development and subsequently a more specific one, sustainable development.

With regard to communication also, a major shifts has taken place from top-down authoritative model of communication to a two way horizontal and participatory model of communication.

Significance of the Research Study

There have been many studies carried out on development and communication, media and development, environment and media, environment and communication and communication, rural development and communication media, traditional folk-media and development and participatiory development communication. But, though sustainable development is the latest and present trend of development, sofar, proper attention has not been paid to this area from communication point of view. Therefore, it has been felt worthwhile to study the role of communication for sustainable rural development.

Research Questions

Sustainable development being the latest and the present trend of development, the broad aim of the study is to analyze the role of communication in sustainable development and to recommend a communication strategy for sustainable development.

Objectives of this Study

(*a*) To identify the implications of sustainable rural development.

(*b*) To find out the policies and programmes of Indian Government towards sustainable development.

(*c*) To study and analyze the role of communication in sustainable rural development.

(*d*) An empirical study has been intended to be carried out in a backward and environmentally affected district in Orissa:

The following aspects were sought to be examined in Koraput, Orissa.

A. Role of Communication in the success or failure of poverty alleviation programmes;

B. Awareness about environment, Family Planning and reflection of that awareness in their lifestyles;

C. Source of information to people and their media habits;

D. Role played by various communication media in relation to combating pollution and in connection with environmental movements;

E. To recommend a communication strategy for sustainable development.

Research Methodology

This study is based on both primary and secondary data. The secondary data has been collected from the books, reports, journals, magazines, newspapers, government records and seminar papers.

The primary data has been collected on two broad areas:

(*a*) Communication and poverty alleviation programmes;

(*b*) Environmental awareness and media habits among the people of Koraput distric.

For the study of the role of communication, in the success or failure of the poverty alleviation programmes, two villages viz., Nandapur and Pottangi were selected from two revenue divisions of Koraput district. In these villages, information is collected from the target beneficiaries of IRDP and DWCRA schemes. The respondents include both beneficiaries of these schemes. 100 respondents from each of these two villages were selected through systematic random sampling.

Role of Management Communication for Sustainable Development

Communication is a basic instinct of man. It is the fact of life of not only human beings, but also of animals, birds and other living beings. Communication maintains and animates life. It is also the expression of social activity and civilization. It leads people from instincts to inspiration through various processes and systems of enquiry, command and control.

Communication integrates knowledge, organizations and power and runs a thread linking the earliest memory of man to his noblest aspiration through constant thriving for a better life. As the world has advanced, the task of communication has become ever more complex and subtle to liberate mankind from want, oppression and four and to write it in community and communion, solidarity and understanding.

Mass communication comprise the institutions and technology by which specialized groups employ technological devices(press, radio, films etc.) to disseminate symbolic content to large, heterogeneous and widely dispersed audiences.

Poverty eradication, protecting the environment, reducing the consumption of non-renewable resources and increasing the use of renewable resources, conservation of biological diversity, controlling various types of pollution, land degradation and deforestation, waste management using appropriate technologies, land reforms, population control and stabilization, upholding basic human rights, social welfare and woman's upliftment, promoting intra-generational and intergenerational equity and participation of people from individual, local levels to global level, being the various important objectives of sustainable development , different communication channels have a potential role to play in fulfilling these objectives. Though communication alone is not sufficient to meet these objectives. It is a crucial element in facilitating the fulfillment of these objectives.

Management Communication Policy and Strategy

Strategies that include management communication for sustainable rural development as a significant aspect of agricultural and rural development are sorely needed. Efforts in this direction are being made, but governments have yet to recognize fully the potential of this factor in promoting public awareness and information on agricultural innovations, as well as on the planning and development of small business, not to mention employment opportunities and basic news about health, education and other factors of concern to rural populations, particularly those seeking to improve their livelihoods and thereby enhance the quality of their lives.

Rural development is often discussed together with agricultural development and agricultural extension. In fact 'agricultural extension' is often termed 'rural extension' in the literature. In contrast, rural development includes but nonetheless expands beyond the confines of agriculture, and furthermore requires and also involves developments other than agriculture. Accordingly, government should consider the establishment of a communication policy that while supporting agricultural extension for rural development also assumes the role of a 'rural extension' service aimed as well at diffusing non-agricultural information and advice to people in rural areas.

A communication policy would aim to systematically promote rural communication activities, especially interactive radio but also other successful media such as tape recorder and video instructional programmes. Computers and the Internet may not yet be accessible to rural communities but they serve the communication intermediaries and agricultural extension agents who provide information to rural populations. Other devices such as cell phones hold considerable promise for the transfer and exchange of practical information.

For reaching the final agricultural and basic needs information users in rural areas today, radio is the most powerful and cost-effective medium. However, other traditional and modern communication methods are equally valuable, depending on the situation and availability, like face-to-face exchanges (via demonstration and village meetings); one-way print media (such as, newspapers, newsletters, magazines, journals, posters); one-way telecommunication media (including non-interactive radio, television, satellite, computer, cassette, video and loudspeakers mounted on cars); and two-way media: (telephone, including teleconferencing, and interactive (Internet) computer).

Information and communication technologies (ICTs) have proved to be important for Internet users and for the intermediate users who work with the poor. Pilot experiences show that various media are valuable for assisting agricultural producers with information and advice as to agricultural innovations, market prices, pest infestations and weather alerts.

ICTs also serve non-farming rural people with information and advice regarding business opportunities relating to food processing, wholesale outlets and other income-generating opportunities. In the case of non-agricultural rural development interests, a communication for rural development policy would aim to promote diffusion of information about non-agricultural micro-enterprise development, small business planning, nutrition, health and generally serve to provide useful, other-than-agriculture information.

By its very nature as mass media, communication for rural development can provide information useful to all segments of rural populations. However, it would serve as a first effort toward advancement of 'rural extension' services and activities aimed at rural development concerns beyond those of agriculture. Thus, extension and communication activities would be expected to work in tandem, allied in the common cause of supporting income-generating activities, both agricultural and non-agricultural.

Managing Communication for Awareness

Awareness among people is one of the primary requirements for the success of any programme relating to sustainable development whether it is a poverty alleviation programme of family planning programme or afforestation programme, people should be aware of it, its importance and its utility.

For the success of poverty alleviation programmes and for environmental protection, communication is an essential ingredient. It plays a key role in preparing people to make various programmes relating to sustainable rural development.

Communication has a great role to play in creating awareness pertaining to various aspects of sustainable development. Different communication channels can create awareness at different levels. At global, national, or regional levels mass media have a great role to play in creating awareness. At local levels various governmental and non-governmental organizations NGOs) have a significant role in creating awareness among people.

Mass Education and Management Communication

Communication has a potent role to play in sustainable development by educating people, providing more details and explaining complexities. The most relevant in this content is the Chinese perception about education which says' if you plan for one year, plant a rice, if you plan for ten years, plant trees, if you plan for one hundred years, educate the people."

The chief objectives of environmental education is that individual and social groups should acquire awareness and knowledge, develop attitudes, skills and abilities and participate in solving real life environmental problems. The perception of environmental education should be integrated interdisciplinary and holistic in character.

Conclusion

The discussion mentioned above shows that though there are many definitions and multiple dimensions to sustainable development, these definitions and dimensions are not contradictory to each other but they corroborate each other. Broadly, the sustainable development can be described as the poverty alleviation i.e. to enable the present generations to meet their needs and environmental protection to enable the future generations to meet their needs. In relation to communication, it implies that communication in general and various communication channels in particular have a vital role to play in creating awareness about the various poverty alleviation programmes initiated by the government; in the problem articulated by poor, and thus, in bridging the gap between the planner and the beneficiary.

Environmental protection and promotion and population control being the other broad dimensions of sustainable development, various communication channels have a responsible role to play in informing, educating and conscientizing the people about various environmental issues and promotional programmes—sustainable use of natural resources, using renewable sources of energy, conservation of biological diversity, waste management, prevention and control of pollution, family planning, etc. Besides, communication is of vital importance in promoting human rights, gender equality, social welfare and peace. Since the sustainable development calls for the participation of people—individuals,. national and international levels, various communication channels are of great importance in facilitating the participation of people from individual, local levels to global level. Besides, since sustainable development calls for a lifestyle that is equitable and environment-friendly in moulding such lifestyle throughout the globe, communication has a potential role to play.

References

Kumar, Keval J., *Mass Communication in India,* Bombay : Jaico Publishing House, 1987.

Desai,Vasant, *Rural Development,* Vol. 1. Himalaya Publishing House, 1988.

Kuppuswamy, B., *Communication and Social Development in India,* Bombay: Media Promoters and Publishers Pvt. Ltd., 2000.

McBride Sean., UNESCO International Commission for the Study of Communication Problems, *Many Voices One World,* UNESCO, 1980.

Maheswari Henry et al(2005); *Learning from the Rural Poor,* Indian Social Institute, New Delhi.

Wang Georgette and Wimal Dissanayake, *"The Study of Indigenous Communication Systems on Development: Phased out or Phasing in Media Asia,* Vol. 9, Number 1, 1982, p. 3.

CHAPTER

Management of Stress and Performance

*Dr. (Ms.) Subhashree Panda

Introduction

To survive in these competitive times, creating a high performance organization requires understanding what factors influence performance. One of the most significant factors is stress. The theory of optimal arousal states that performance is best when the arousal level is medium. This concept has been applied by Walter Gmelch (1982) in his book, *Beyond Stress to Effective Management.* Historically, stress has been viewed as an inevitable consequence of work life; or at most, a health care issue. Neither view begins to capture just how costly this problem is to employers. Research shows that stress interferes with human intellectual, emotional, and interpersonal functioning. Initiatives like the Learning Organization, Process Re-engineering, Diversity Training, Collaborative Team Work, and the High Performance Organization are all impacted by the way people are affected by stress.

* Lecturer, Department of Business Administration, North Orissa University, Baripada, Orissa

Positive and Negative Effects of Stress

Selye (1974, 1978) uses two separate terms 'Eustress' and 'Distress' to distinguish between positive and negative consequences of stress for the individual. Eustress is defined as the healthy, positive, constructive outcome of stressful events and stress response. Eustress is the stress of achievement, triumph, and exhilaration. Distress, on the other hand, is the degree of physiological, psychological and behavioural deviation from healthy functioning (Quick et. al., 1997). According to Norfolk (1977), when stress is handled effectively it provides the motivation, which provides encouragement to overcome the obstacles that separate an individual from his hopes and goals. Sometimes, the pressures and demands that may cause stress can be positive in their effect. One example of this is where sportsmen and women flood their bodies with fight-or-flight adrenaline to power an explosive performance. Another example is where deadlines are used to motivate people who seem bored or unmotivated.

In most work situations jobs, our stress response causes our performance to suffer. A calm, rational, controlled and sensitive approach is usually called for in dealing with most difficult problems at work. Our social inter-relationships are just too complex not to be damaged by an aggressive approach, while a passive and withdrawn response to stress means that we can fail to assert our rights when we should. As we become uncomfortably stressed, distractions, difficulties, anxieties and negative thinking begin to crowd our minds. This is particularly the case, when a person perceives that "demands exceed the personal and social resources the individual is able to mobilize." These thoughts compete with performance of the task for our attentional capacity. Concentration suffers, and focus narrows as our brain becomes overloaded. The more our brain is overloaded, the more our performance can suffer.

Stress and the Loss of Creativity

When animals, including human beings, are exposed to potentially life threatening situations; their bodies release endorphins, which are nature's pain-killer. This sets the stage for serious intellectual and interpersonal consequences; because endorphins dull both our ability to think and our ability to feel. Effective decision-making and interpersonal skills require both.

Creative and innovative thought is at the heart of the learning organization. An organization's ability to innovate is the most important source of competitive advantage. Organizations who know how to stimulate and leverage innovative thought are able to respond more rapidly and resourcefully to market changes and customer requirements than their slower, less innovative competitors. Despite the tremendous contribution innovative thought makes to organizational survival, most organizations don't realize how they prevent such thought from being exercised in their organization.

Studies show that when people are under stress, their thought processes narrow. This narrowing of attention prevents divergent thinking, which is the foundation of creativity. Divergent thinking is the ability to see connections between very distantly related ideas and context. It is an important component of 'thinking outside the box.' When people are stressed, they are able to perceive obvious connections and associations between ideas. When people are in a positive emotional state, their ability to make more distant, novel connections and associations increases. Thus, stress compromises, at the most fundamental neurological level, one of the foundational skills of creativity and innovation.

Effects of Stress on Performance

The impact of organsational stress on well being and performance is extensively documented (Cooper &

Marshall,1976, 1978; Beehr and Newman, 1978; Cherniss,1980; Quick and Quick, 1984). The beneficial and deleterious effects of stress on performance and efficiency were first described in 1908 by Yerkes and Dodson of the Harvard Physiologic Laboratory. These investigations demonstrated that as stress increases, efficiency and performance also increase. However, this relation persists only up to a certain level. If stress increases beyond this level, performance and efficiency decrease.

The relationship between stress and performance is shown in Fig. 6.1. In terms of influence of varying degrees of stress

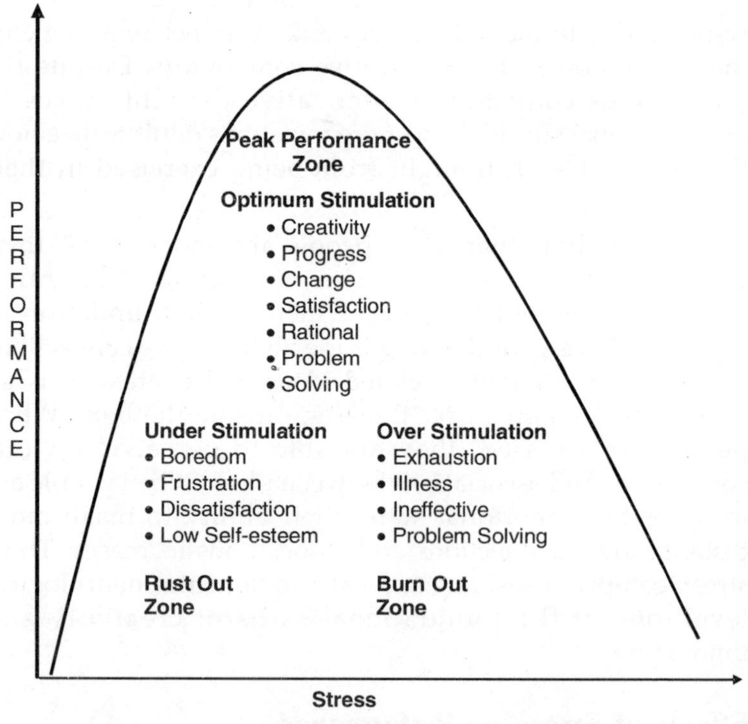

Fig. 6.1. Effects of Stress on Performance
(*Source:* Kindler and Ginsberg, 1990)

on individuals, three zones have been identified. When there is minimum stress one experiences boredom and is said to be in the comfort zone. Stretch zone is the area of peak performance, where we feel stimulated, energised and confident and function in a resourceful, successful state (William, 1994). The successful management of stress is based on one's awareness, acceptance of responsibility and action in initiating and managing the forces (external or internal) causing stress. In other words, burnout occurs when there is over stress or hyper stress and one has exceeded one's limits of adaptability to cope with the stress. On the other hand, rust out is when there is lack of self realization due to very low level of stress which is termed as hypostress or understress. Both hyper and hypo stress can be equally destructive in the long-run.

Research Findings on Stress and Performance

Although several authors posit a negative linear relationship between stress and performance, other evidence suggests that this relationship is actually an inverted-U shape. This hypothesis suggests that individual performance on a given task will be lower at high and low levels of stress and optimal at moderate levels of stress. At moderate levels of stress, performance is likely to be improved by the presence of enough stimulation to keep the individual vigilant and alert, but not enough to divert or absorb his energy and focus. At low levels of stress, in contrast, activation and alertness may be too low to foster effective performance, while at high levels of stress, arousal is too high to be conductive to task performance.

Research findings suggest that when an individual comes under stress, his cognitive performance and decision-making may be adversely affected. Notably, under conditions of stress, individuals are likely to

- Screen out peripheral stimuli (Easterbrook, 1959; Janis and Mann, 1977; Staw, Sandelands, and Dutton, 1981).

- Make decisions based on heuristics (rules of thumb or guidelines) (Shaham, Singer, and Schaeffer, 1992; Klein, 1996).
- Suffer from performance rigidity or narrow thinking (Friedman and Mann, 1993; Keinan, 1987).
- Lose their ability to analyze complicated situations and manipulate information (Larsen, 2001).

Also, researchers have found that task completion time may be increased and accuracy reduced by stress (Idzikowski and Baddeley, 1983; McLeod, 1977). In addition to effects on the individual, stress has also been shown to negatively affect group functioning. When stressed, individuals are likely to yield control to their superiors and to allow authority to become more concentrated in the upper levels of the hierarchy. Communication effectiveness may also be reduced (Driskell, Carson, and Moskal, 1988). Stress can also lead to 'groupthink,' in which members of the group ignore important cues, force all members to adhere to a consensus decision—even an incorrect one—and rationalize poor decisions (Janis and Mann, 1977).

Even if some level of stress may have a positive effect on performance as suggested by the U-hypothesis, extended exposure to stress or a single exposure to an extreme stressor can have severe negative consequences on non-task performance dimensions. For example, high levels of stress can lead to emotional exhaustion, lower organizational commitment, and increased turnover intentions (Cropanzano, Rapp, and Bryne, 2003). In extreme cases, stress can lead to post-traumatic stress disorder (PTSD), a psychiatric illness that can interfere with life functioning. PTSD has a variety of symptoms, including flashbacks, difficulty in sleeping, and social isolation.

There is an increasing awareness of the importance of stress and its effects on the personal and organizational effectiveness (Beehr & Newman, 1978). Although stress can be both pleasant (eustress) and unpleasant (distress) (Betnard,1968), a substantial body of research indicates its undesirable outcomes for the individuals and the organization (Kahn et al., 1964; Armenakis, 1981). Allen et.al., (1982) have shown the negative relation of stress with perceived organizational effectiveness. On the other hand, Singh & Singh (1984) and Mishra (1984) have found a positive and significant relationship of stress with job involvement.

Kate de Vries (1979), suggests that each individual needs a moderate amount of stress to be alert and capable of functioning effectively in an organization. Pestonjee (1987), says that optimum levels of stress lead to achievement, higher productivity and that it is natural and healthy to maintain optimum levels of stress as achievement, higher productivity and effectiveness call for stress. Kallausner (1968) suggests that success in business depends on stress seeking tendencies. However, McLean (1964), has put forth a different view that occupational stress produces maladaptive response, including aversive effects on work performance and on interpersonal relationships.

Srivastava (1983) studied the stress-performance (production) relationship, considering the latter as a determinant of the former rather than vice-versa. The findings of the study established that employees who maintained a constantly high production level by virtue of their attributed productivity, perceived and experienced less role stress as compared to employees with low production capacity. In another study Srivastava, Naidu and Mishra (1986) investigated the relationship between stress and performance. The results of this study supported the predicted inverted U-relationship between stress and performance for only the low impulse control subjects who showed lowest level of performance under high stress conditions. Jamal (1985) on the other hand, reaffirmed the prevalence of a negative linear relationship between job stress and supervisory ratings of performance.

Kindler and Ginsberg (1990), have explained the effects of too little and too high levels of stress on performance. They are of the view that when there is too little stress, performance is also low. When stress level is too high, again performance suffers. Somewhere between these two extremes is the optimum level of stress where one attains peak performance. A large body of literature has documented the consequences of burnout, which is the consequences of prolonged and severe stress. Dougherty (1993, 1996) and Cordes & Dougherty (1993) conclude that burnout has often been associated with diminished levels of performance and with a general withdrawal of the individual from a meaningful psychological involvement with the organization.

Yerkes and Dodson (1908) examined the relationship between stress and performance. Initially a person's performance increases under pressure until an optimum level has been reached. From here, performance begins to decline if more pressure is brought to bear, and, if the pressure is not reduced, performance is impaired and the individual's health may suffer. The way in which stress levels can be optimized will depend on whether the stress is short or long term in nature. Short term stress occurs in situations that are confrontational, sporting events, visiting dentist, giving a speech, and so on, and optimizing stress involves the short-term management of adrenaline to maximize performance. In the long term, where adrenaline has been released over long periods, optimizing stress focuses on the management of health and energy.

Stress and Performance: Possible Relationship Frameworks

Although much of the research on the relationship between stress and functioning focuses on the negative performance effects of stress, not all stress is bad. In fact, Selye (1956) emphasizes that stress is a necessary part of life and that it does not always involve negative consequences for the organism involved. In fact, at certain moderate levels, stress can actually improve individual performance. There is substantial research supporting the concept of 'good stress.' Yerkes and Dodson (1908) were the first to 'stumble' upon the inverted-U relationship between stress and performance. Their work focused on the effects of stress on the learning response of rats. Using three trials with low, moderate, and high levels of stimulus, they find a weak but curvilinear relationship, with performance on the task improving as the stressor stimulus reached a moderate level and decreasing as stimulus strength increased beyond this point.

Research since Yerkes and Dodson has supported the inverted-U relationship between stress and performance. Scott (1966) finds that individual performance increases with stress and resulting arousal to an optimal point and then decreases as stress and stimulation increase beyond this optimum. Furthermore, Srivastava and Krishna (1991) find evidence that an inverted-U relationship does exist for job performance in the industrial context. Selye (1975) and McGrath (1976) also suggest an inverted-U relationship between stress and performance. Finally, research on arousal theory supports the inverted-U hypothesis, assuming that external stressors produce a stress response that is similar physiologically to arousal. Sanders (1983) and Gaillard and Steyvers (1989) find that performance is optimal when arousal is at moderate levels. When arousal is either too high or too low, performance declines.

There are many critics of the inverted-U hypothesis who argue that the relationship between stress and performance does not have a U-shape. One alternative model is a negative linear relationship. For example, Jamal (1985) argues that stress at any level reduces task performance by draining an individual's energy, concentration, and time. Vroom (1964) offers a similar explanation, suggesting that physiological responses caused by stressors impair performance. Some psychologists even suggest a linear positive relationship between stress and performance. For example, Meglino (1977) argues that at low levels of stress, challenge is absent and performance is poor. Optimal performance in his model comes at the highest level of stress. There have been some studies in support of this hypothesis, including Arsenault and Dolan (1983) and Hatton et al. (1995). Despite the empirical evidence supporting these alternative theories, the inverted-U hypothesis is still the most intuitively appealing and the most used explanation for how stress and performance are related (Muse, Harris, and Field, 2003).

Stress and Decision-making, Perception, and Cognition

Stress can affect an individual's decision-making process and ability to make effective judgments. For example, Easterbrook (1959) proposes a 'cue utilization model' and argues that when exposed to stressors, individuals experience 'perceptual narrowing'—meaning that they pay attention to fewer perceptual cues or stimuli that could contribute to their behaviour or decision. Peripheral stimuli are likely to be the first to be screened out or ignored. Decision-making models proposed by Janis and Mann (1977) support this hypothesis and suggest that under stress, individuals may make decisions based on incomplete information. Friedman and Mann (1993) suggest that when under conditions of stress, individuals may fail to consider the full range of alternatives available, ignore long-term consequences, and make decisions based on oversimplifying assumptions.

Furthermore, the work of Staw, Sandelands, and Dutton (1981) suggests that individuals may suffer from performance rigidity as a result of their reduced search behaviour and reliance on fewer perceptual cues to make decisions. Research on decision-making under stress supports these theoretical models. For example, Wallsten (1980) observes the decision-making processes of individuals under time pressure. He finds that individuals under time pressure tend to focus their attention only on a few salient cues. Keinan (1987) studies the decision-making behaviour of a group of undergraduate students. The students were asked to solve decision problems while being exposed to varying types of stressors. While the type of stressor did not seem to have an effect on decision-making, those students exposed to a stressor were significantly more likely to offer solutions to the computer-generated problems without considering all the alternatives, to scan alternatives in a nonsystematic way, and to have lower quality of performance than those students not exposed to a stressor.

Research by Shaham, Singer, and Schaeffer (1992) suggests that individuals are more likely to use heuristics (rules of thumb or guidelines based on past experience that are used to help in decision-making) when they are faced with external stressors. They compare the heuristic use of two groups of people on a survey, one that was asked to first complete an analytical test while being subjected to loud noises and a second that did not complete the stress-exposure test. These authors find that individuals in the experimental group, who exhibited elevated levels of hostility, anxiety, and irritability after their initial exposure to the stressors, were about 12.5 per cent more likely than the control group to use heuristics while taking the second survey. However, the authors do not look at whether individuals performed better or worse on the analytical test when using heuristics. Klein (1996) also finds that when confronted with external stressors, individuals are more likely to use heuristics and other simplified decision-making strategies. However, rather than reducing the quality of individual decisions, as suggested by those researchers who argue for perceptual narrowing, Klein suggests that the use of heuristics may allow individuals to respond more quickly to external demands and can also help them make effective judgments under some kinds of stressors or with only partial information.

Larsen (2001) looks at the effects of sleep deprivation on individual perception, judgment, and decision-making. He considers a sample of sleep-deprived Norwegian military personnel enrolled in a combat training course. After five days with little or no sleep, these individuals were asked to conduct a simulated nighttime village raid. The individuals had conducted a similar raid before, shooting at cardboard figures meant to represent people. In this particular simulation, the figures were replaced with real people and the students' guns were emptied of ammunition. Larsen finds that, like other types of stressors, sleep deprivation can reduce an individual's ability to reason, to analyze complex situations, and to make effective decisions. Sleep-deprived (stressed) individuals in his study were more likely to obey orders without thinking and to ignore cues that implied the presence of something unusual. In fact, 59 per cent of the students in Larsen's sample fired their weapons several times during the simulation. Half these students reported that they did see movement in the camp—suggesting that something was unusual and that real people might be in the camp—but they fired anyway because they had been told to or because their thinking was too confused to make an effective decision.

Stress can also contribute to performance decrements by slowing cognition and individual information processing. For example, Idzikowski and Baddeley (1983) find that the time to complete a given task doubled with the introduction of an external stressor. McLeod (1977) looks specifically at stress in the form of 'task overload' (e.g., asking an individual to perform more than one task under a time constraint) and finds that the addition of multiple required tasks reduces the quality of individual performance and increases the magnitude of the performance decrement as compared with the case in which the individual has only one task to perform.

Stress and Group Functioning

While the effects of stress on individual performance are relevant, the effects of stress on group functioning are equally important. Bowers, Weaver, and Morgan (1996) argue that group-level stressors can involve any influence of the group on the individual that leads to increased tension or decreased functioning—for example, competition among members or crowding. Group decision-making processes can be affected by the presence of stressors. Most importantly, Driskell, Carson, and Moskal (1988) find that when subjected to stressful conditions, individuals are more likely to yield control to their partners or superiors. As a result, authority tends to become more concentrated and hierarchy more pronounced. In addition, communication within the group may suffer as a result of perceptual narrowing. Cannon-Bowers and Salas (1998) hypothesize that the stimuli lost through perceptual narrowing are those most important to group communication and effectiveness. As a result, the group-level effects of stress may be even more significant than those at the individual level. Stress can also lead to what Janis and Mann (1977) call 'groupthink,' in which members of the group may ignore important cues, force all members to conform or adhere to the consensus opinion, and even rationalize poor decisions.

Stress and Job Satisfaction and Turnover Intentions

Research also suggests that moderate levels of stress can have positive effects on job satisfaction and organizational commitment while reducing turnover intent. These findings seem to be an extension of the inverted-U-shaped relationship discussed previously. Under this hypothesis, at moderate levels of stress, individual performance and productivity are likely to be higher and can also contribute to higher job satisfaction and organizational commitment. For example, Zivnuska, Kiewitz, and Hochwarter (2002) find that moderate levels of stress tend to be correlated with higher levels of job satisfaction than either very high or very low stress levels. The moderate stress is perceived as stimulating and challenging, without being unbearable. Empirically, the authors demonstrate the non-linear relationship of stress with turnover intent, value attainment, and job satisfaction by including a tension-squared term as a predictor variable in their model. They find that the tension-squared term has a statistically significant relationship with each of the outcome variables. These findings suggest that turnover intent increases quadratically with job tension, while value attainment and job satisfaction decrease quadratically with tension.

These findings are supported by the work of Milgram, Orenstein, and Zafrir (1989), which looks at the effects of stress on a group of Israeli soldiers. They find that moderate levels of stress foster increased group cooperation, commitment, and morale, all of which can contribute to effective group performance. As stress levels decline from the 'optimal' level, the authors find that individual endorsement of official goals of the military, military unit morale, and loyalty to the unit also decline. Taken together, these studies suggest that although stress often comes along with a negative connotation in popular language, it does exist in positive and helpful forms that can contribute to individual and group intensity and achievement. This type of stress is likely to be particularly important for military personnel in peacekeeping deployments, where a certain level of stress may help maintain vigilance and reduce boredom.

Long-term Effects of Stress

However, while exposure to some level of stressor may help individual performance, the long-term effects of stress on the individual tend to be negative, according to the majority of research looking at prolonged exposure to stress. One potential result of an extended exposure to a single or to multiple stressors is burnout, defined by Maslach, Schaufeli, and Leiter (2001) to include exhaustion, feelings of cynicism and detachment, a sense of ineffectiveness, and lack of accomplishment. Burnout is most often measured on the Maslach Burnout Inventory (MBI). Individuals with high MBI scores tend to exhibit higher levels of job dissatisfaction and lower workplace effectiveness. Work by Lee and Ashforth (1990) supports the argument that high and consistent exposure to stress can lead to burnout. They find that psychological strain and burnout have a correlation of 0.94 and that physiological strain and burnout have a correlation of 0.56. Although this does not imply a causal relationship, it does support the argument that individual stress levels are strongly related to burnout.

Long-term exposure to stressors can also have other negative effects. For example, Cropanzano, Rapp, and Bryne (2003) find that long term exposure to high levels of stressors can lead to emotional exhaustion, which has been shown to degrade organizational commitment and increase turnover intentions. According to Seymour and Black (2002), chronic stress can also lead to physical problems, including cardiovascular disease, muscle pain, stomach and intestinal problems, decreased fertility, and reduced immune system strength. Long-term stress can also lead to feelings of anger, anxiety, fatigue, depression, and sleep problems.

In the extreme, long-term exposure to high levels of stressors or a single exposure to a very demanding event can lead to Post-Traumatic Stress Disorder(PTSD), a psychiatric illness that can interfere with life functioning. PTSD has a variety of symptoms, including nightmares, flashbacks, difficulty sleeping, and social isolation. Not all individuals who experience extreme stress will develop PTSD, though factors that make individuals more or less susceptible to PTSD include the type of stressor experienced, genetics, lack of social support, or the existence of other mental or physical diseases (Green et al., 1990; Kahana, Harel, and Kahana, 1988; Adler, Vaitkus, and Martin, 1996). Combat experience is one of the types of stressors that can bring on PTSD. In fact, PTSD has been observed in nearly all veteran populations studied, including those who served in World War II, the Korean War, Persian Gulf conflicts, and UN peacekeeping deployments. Specifically, for the Vietnam War, a study conducted 15 years after the end of the conflict found that at least 15 per cent of veterans were still suffering from PTSD symptoms (Schlenger et al., 1992).

Uncontrollable Stress and the Dumbing Down Process

Research by Dr. James Pennebaker of Southern Methodist University has demonstrated a very serious consequence of uncontrollable stress on thought processes. In an experiment performed by Dr. Pennebaker, subjects wrote about whatever was going on in their mind — their 'stream of consciousness.' One group was subjected to a loud noise in the middle of the exercise and told there was nothing they could do about it; they had to 'grin and bear it.' The other group was subjected to the same loud noise in the middle of the exercise, but they were told they could have the noise stopped if they chose. The results were both fascinating and disturbing in their implications for organizational performance.

The group that had no control demonstrated a significant deterioration in their thought process during and after the noise. Their thinking became unemotional, unimaginative, and dull. It was as if they became temporarily dumb in order to endure the stressful situation. Even more interesting was the other group's response, although they were told they could stop the noise if they needed to, not one person chose to do so. Therefore, they experienced the same amount of unpleasant noise as the group which wasn't given that option.

Despite being subjected to the same amount of noxious noise, their thought process remained unaffected. They engaged in deep, reflective, creative thought. Thus, it wasn't the negative external situation, but the perceived lack of control, which resulted in a diminished thinking capacity. The operative term here is perceived. This study and others like it show that even if a person's perception is wrong — if in fact they really don't have control, the effect is the same as if they truly had control. It's the perception, the belief, that matters.

Implications for the Workplace

In workplaces where people are constantly afraid and insecure, employees are at risk of 'numbing out' to protect themselves. We see it in the blank faces of clerks, the lack of enthusiasm by front line workers, and in the remarkably insensitive ways managers and employees treat each other. The very mechanism which allows a person to survive an emotionally painful environment also makes it difficult for them to respond sensitively and empathetically to others. The organizational conflict and customer service consequences of this are obviously very costly.

This numbing process affects far more than the interpersonal realm of organizational performance. It affects all aspects of decision-making, innovation, and safety. With their thinking impaired, people are at greater risk of causing serious mistakes and accidents. They are also obviously less likely to make wise decisions and create process improvements.

Employee intellectual functioning can be very powerfully influenced by their environment. In workplaces where employees feel helpless and disempowered, they are less likely to think in intelligent, creative ways. Another important implication, and this is born out by other research, is that perceived control plays a major role in whether a person is affected by a potentially stressful workplace. Workers in jobs with similar demands, but different levels of control, exhibit very different psychological and physiological responses. With the same demand level, workers in low control workplaces are significantly more affected by their work. Thus, when workers have little control over their work and feel powerless in general, they are more likely to suffer from the kind of 'dumbing down' that Pennebaker's work demonstrated.

In thinking about organizational implications, we need to realize that the word 'perceived' in the term, 'perceived control' is important. It is important because in reality, there is no way we can create a workplace in which a person has total control over their work and over their destiny. No organization can guarantee life-long employment, no one can foresee market changes or economic downturns. But, as long as people have open lines of communication and know that they can get the information they need—even if it's 'we don't know yet,' they experience a sense of control. Thus, organizations which enable open, honest communication create a context in which people are less likely to be stressed out, and because of that, more likely to utilize their capabilities.

Conclusion

Stress is a fact of life, and it is important to learn how to use stress constructively to improve performance. Although stressors will almost certainly have a physiological effect on individual (such as increasing heart rate) and will likely have some negative effect on their performance of complex tasks, the application of moderators, including training and provision of additional information, can help individuals to adapt successfully to challenging stressors and maintain high levels of performance. To create a high performance organization, an organization which brings out the best in its people, we need to understand how stress affects people's intellectual, emotional, and interpersonal functioning. By drawing on the wealth of research available, we can make recommendations which increase the probability that people will not be compromised by stress, but instead, perform at optimal levels.

References

Chauhan, Daisy, *Managing Executive Stress : An Approach to Self Development*, Excel Books, New Delhi, 2002, pp. 90-93.

Edworthy, Ann, *Managing Stress*, Open University Press, Philadelphia, 2000. p. 8.

Ganguli, Siddarhata, *Performance Management :First Time Right*, Platinum Publisher,.Kolkata,2009, pp.271-281.

http://www.mindtools.com/stress/UnderstandStress/StressPerformance.htm

http://www. rand .org.

http://www.dushkin.com/connectext/psy/ch12/streper.mhtml

http://www.humannatureatwork.com/Workplace-Stress-2.ht

Stephen P. Robbins, *Organizational Behaviour: Concepts, Controversies Applic*ations, Prentice Hall of India Private Limited, New Delhi, 1996, pp. 611- 618.

CHAPTER

Management of Organisational Behaviour

*Rajib Lochan Panigrahy
**Anil Kumar Sahu

Introduction to Management

Management is a process of taking things done by the people. It is a process of taking managerial decision and putting them into action. It is concerned with motivation of the employees. Management is the brain of an organization which helps to take decision, makes policies, rules and regulations with the concern of factors of production i.e. men, machine, money, material and method. It is concerned with motivation of employees. The success of an organization depends on the optimum utilization of resources in an effective way. Every organization requires taking of decision, coordination activities of workers, handling people, evaluation of performance of those directed towards attainment of objectives. This is possible only when there will be a good relationship between master-servant, employee-employer, manager and staff prevails. It requires high degree of professional, technical ability and managerial abilities. Management requires tackling of complex business problem effectively and efficiently towards the organizational goals. Hence, management is defined by different authors as:

> "Management is getting things done through and with people in formally organized groups. It is the art of creating an environment in which people can perform as individual and yet cooperate towards achievement of group goals". —*Harold Koontz*

> "Management may be defined as the art of securing maximum prosperity with minimum of efforts so as to secure maximum prosperity and happiness for both employer and employee and give the public the best possible service". —*John F.Mee*

> "To manage is to forecast and plan, to organize, to command, to coordinate and to control." —*Henry Fayol*

Management is important for our society, organizations, industries. Organisation or industry is a group of activities. So, the organization should make the internal environment conducive, so that the people at work can perform their job better. Management activities are meant to achieve common goals by establishing good relations to the personnel working in the organization and the good relation among them which depends on the manager or the top management personnel behaviour. It establishes good relationship among resources. So,

> "Good management is the art of making problem so interesting and their solutions so constructive that everyone wants to get to work and deal with them."
>
> —*Paul Hawken*

Introduction to OB

From the above discussions it is found that management is a creative problem solving process. It involves four to five kinds of managerial functions as planning, organizing, staffing, directing and controlling following certain skills to perform that basic objectives. Organisational behaviour is an applied behavioural skill that are built on contributions from a number of behavioural disciplines. It requires different management skills as technical skill, human skills and conceptual skills to be carried out by the managers. The managers may be top level, middle level or line managers. They carry the technical skills with techniques of utilizing the things, human skill deals with people, conceptual skill deals with ideas. Managers also deals with interpersonal aspects with providing information, informational aspects makes process information, decisional roles for use of information. All the things done by managers are taking the help of group activities which depends on the motivation, leadership, interpersonal skills, etc. The managers are sole responsible for this. As the environment they create and maintain in the organization through motivation by the managers, so the effectiveness of the organization. To create and maintain good environment in the organization, the behaviour of the organization should be responsible for which keeps good industrial relation among the workers. The good relation among workers, stakeholders, customers makes the organisation progressive.

Hence, Organisational Behaviour is a systematic study of the actions and attitudes that people exhibit within organization. It deals with individual and group behaviour in organization. OB primarily depends on psychological, interpersonal and behavioural dynamics in organization on the definition of Stephen P. Robbins, "OB is a field of study that investigates the impact of individual, groups and structures of behaviour within organizations for the purpose of applying such knowledge towards improving an organization's effectiveness." This definition envisages the study of behaviour in organization of individuals, groups, structures. It is the common body of knowledge applies to the individuals, groups and the structures on behaviour in order to make organization work more effectively. It deals with the determinants of behaviour in the organization. It should emphasis behaviour as related to job/work, absenteeism, employee turnover, productivity, performance and management. An effective process of organizational behaviour can improve efficiency, ability of work related aspects like job satisfaction, low employee turnover, less absenteeism, accelerate productivity of workers, challenging job handling, good motive workers. A good organisational behaviour develops basic knowledge, special skill and abilities, application knowledge and technical utilisation skill.

To sum up these things, OB is concerned with the study of what people do in an organisation and how their behaviour affects the organisation's performance. OB is specifically concerned with employee related problems. OB includes the core topics of motivation, leadership behaviour, power and politics, inter-personal communication, group structure and processes, learning, attitude, development and perception, change process, conflict, work design, work stress.

Model on Organisational Behaviour

A model is an abstraction of reality, a simplified representative of some real world phenomenon. There are three levels of analysis in OB, there is individual, group and organisational.

Individual ⟶ Group ⟶ Organisational

Fig. 7.1

The three basic levels are analogous to building blocks each level is constructed on previous level. Individual section paid foundation for group level concept and the group has constructed organisational system with individuals.

There are two variables attracting OB model, they are dependant variables and independent which affects OB which are described below.

Dependant Variables of OB

1. Productivity : Productivity implies a concern for both effectiveness and efficiency of the goal achieved with transferring input and output at a lower cost. Productivity is effective when it successfully meets the needs of its customers it is effective when it can do so at a low cost. The factors will influence the effectiveness and efficiency of individuals, groups and of the overall organisation.

2. Absenteeism : It is defined as the failure of reporting to work. And it is a huge cost and disruption to employees. It is difficult for an organisation to operate smoothly to attain its objectives if employees fail to report at work. Absenteeism results a drastic reduction in quality of output, production, goods and services and also be a complete shutdown of production. With good organisational behaviour and culture the absenteeism can be checked.

3. Employee Turnover : It is the voluntary or involuntary permanent withdrawal from an organisation. A high turnover results incurring high cost of recruitment, selection, training and it occurs shortage of manpower which affects on production and quality of goods and services. High turnover often looses good, efficient, effective, talent manpower. The good organisational behaviour and culture can check the rate of the over and can retain talents.

4. Deviant work place behaviour : The deviations in organisational at work place increases absenteeism and employ turnover. So the organisational behaviour should be as such which should not be the cause of dissatisfaction of the employees. Deviating organisational behaviour deteriorates employee morale towards work and workplace which may cause violence, accidents, etc. So deviant work place behaviour is otherwise called as anti-social behaviour or work place incivility. It violates the social significant organisational norms and threatens the well being of the organisation or its members working for it.

5. Organisational citizenship behaviour (OCB) : It is a discretionary behaviour that is not part of an employee's formal job requirements. But, that nevertheless promotes the effective functioning of the organisation. Successful organisation need employees who will do more than their usual duties who can provide performance beyond expectations, Modern dynamic organisation needs employees to engage in good citizenship behaviour which helps others for team work, maintain social environment social environment, volunteering for extra work or to help others, avoid unnecessary conflict, respecting spirit to rules and regulations of organisation, graceful tolerance to occasional work-related nuisance or disturbance.

6. **Job satisfaction** : A positive feeling about one's job resulting from an evaluation of its characters. Job satisfaction represents an attitude rather than a behaviour. A good organisational behaviour, organisational culture make the employees satisfied and makes their morale towards effectiveness and efficiency at work. It is find that satisfied worker are more productive than others those who are less satisfied or dissatisfied on job and work place which causes absenteeism, conflict, turnover, etc. Satisfaction at job make the employees efficient, talented, efficient. Satisfaction is an important dependent variable for an organisation to be productive. Hence, it is said that "Happy workers are productive workers."

Independent Variable

An independent variable is the presumed cause of some change in dependent variable.

1. **Individual level** : When people entered into organisations with certain intact characteristics that will influence their behaviour at work. The personal or biographical characteristics, emotional characteristics value, inherent emotional characteristics, values and attitudes, basic ability level, etc. Theses characteristics are essential in workplace but management can alter them on organisational behaviour towards organisation other individual level variables which can affect employee behaviour such as perception, individual decision making , learning and motivation.

2. **Group level :** The individual working in the organisation are associated to be a group. Their behaviour is in group and individual. Therefore, OB is the step for development of behaviour of employees in organisation in group. The good communication among individual in the group will accelerate group behaviour in the organisation with effective leadership, conflict management, it is OB which can do possible.
3. **Organisational System level :** OB reaches to a highest level with individual and group behaviour. Group is a sum of individuals. An organisation may be a group. The organisation culture, its human resource policies and practices. Selection, recruitment, placement, promotion, education and development, performance appraisal and evaluation are the independent variable which affect the organisation system level as dependent variable.

OB—An Applied Behaviour

OB is an applied behavioural science which built on contributions from a number of behavioural disciplines on the predominant areas of psychological, social psychology, sociology, anthropology. Contributions of psychology are mainly on individual or on micro level analysis but the other areas contribute on macro level concepts such as group process and organisation. The areas or disciplines are also sub-divided as :

Psychology : The characteristic as learning, motivation, personality, emotions, perceptions, training, effectiveness of leadership, job satisfaction, individual decision making, performance appraisal, attitude measurement, employee selection, work design, work stress come under the psychology level of OB.

Social Psychology : Behavioural change, change in attitude, communication, group processes, group decision making fell into the social psychology level of OB.

Sociology : Communication, power and politics, conflict, inter-group conflict, formal organisation theory, organisational technology, organisational change, organisational culture are the sociology level of OB.

Anthropology : Comparative values, comparative attitudes, cross-culture analysis, organisational culture, power, organisational environment are the characteristics of OB under anthropology category.

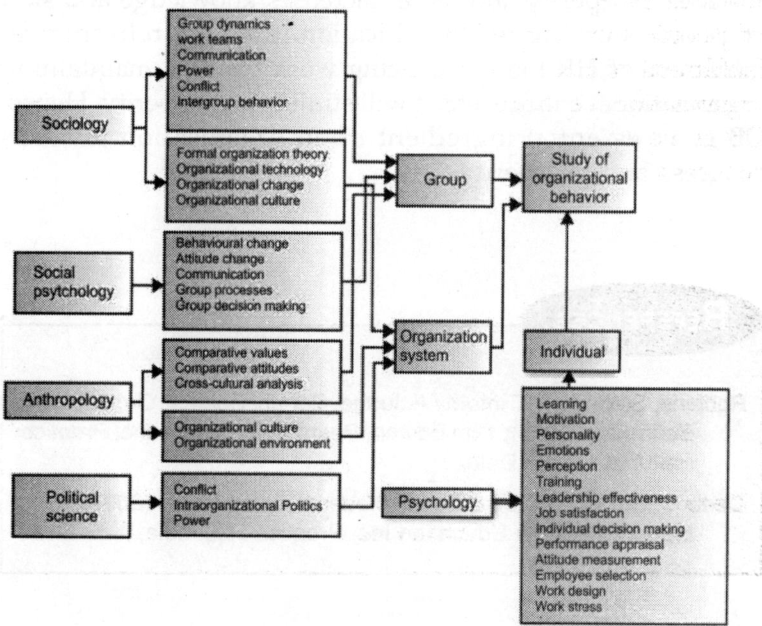

Fig. 7. 2 : Model on Organisation Behaviour

This is the model of correlation of basic organisational behaviour among three levels i.e. individual, group, organisational system level. The flow of activities and linkages has been envisaged on OB has been depicted in the flow chart or diagram.

Conclusion

The manager has to develop interpersonal skills to be effective on job of the individuals, group towards effectiveness and prosperity of the organisation giving much attention to the OB side of the organisational system. Because the behaviour of the organisational system has an impact on individuals, groups and the structure in the organisation in a similar way. OB uses situational variables to moderate cause and effect relationship. OB offers challenges, opportunities for the managers. When the manager empowers its workers, improves customer service and relation, marches ahead towards prosperity and fame, increases knowledge and skill of people working for by education, training, refreshment, fulfilment of HR tools, balancing work conflict, maintaining organisational culture, etc. it will stimulate prosperity. Hence, OB is an essential ingredient of an organisation towards progress and prosperity.

References

Robbins, Stephen P., Timothy A.Judge, Sanghi Seema, *Organisation Behaviour* (2007), 12th Edition, Pearson Education Inc, Prentice Hall India, New Delhi

Certo C. Samal. S.Trevis Certo, *Modern Management* (2007), 10th Edition, Pearson Education Inc, Prentice Hall India, New Delhi

Index

N

O

P

S

T

V

W